T0149514

Why You Didn't Get the Job

TEN STEPS FOR SUCCESS IN BUSINESS
A Woman's Guide to Navigating Her Way to the Top

Diane Cashin
President & CEO
True North Enterprise

authorHOUSE®

AuthorHouse™
1663 Liberty Drive
Bloomington, IN 47403
www.authorhouse.com
Phone: 1-800-839-8640

© *2012 Diane Cashin. All rights reserved.*

*No part of this book may be reproduced, stored in a retrieval system, or
transmitted by any means without the written permission of the author.*

Published by AuthorHouse   10/11/12

ISBN: 978-1-4772-7425-5 (sc)
ISBN: 978-1-4772-7424-8 (dj)
ISBN: 978-1-4772-7423-1 (e)

Library of Congress Control Number: 2012918223

*Any people depicted in stock imagery provided by Thinkstock are models,
and such images are being used for illustrative purposes only.
Certain stock imagery © Thinkstock.*

This book is printed on acid-free paper.

*Because of the dynamic nature of the Internet, any web addresses or links contained in
this book may have changed since publication and may no longer be valid. The views
expressed in this work are solely those of the author and do not necessarily reflect the
views of the publisher, and the publisher hereby disclaims any responsibility for them.*

Contents

Dedication

To all the business leaders who believed in me.

To those who blocked my path for without you, I would not have uncovered these important steps on my journey.

To all women who want to make it to the top, I believe in you and share these steps so you may live your dreams.

To my wonderful family for their love and support.

To David for being with me every step of the way.

To my children, Paul and Samantha, who are my True North.

Disclaimer

The purpose of *Why You Didn't Get the Job* is to consolidate the wisdom, experiences and roadblocks that come up consistently in conversations with women who have aspirational goals of climbing the ladder of success and seek to understand why their career has plateaued. *Why You Didn't Get The Job* empowers all women to accelerate their way to executive-level positions by removing these roadblocks and sharing direct, candid and sometimes-uncomfortable insights women need to understand in order to create breakthroughs and land their next promotion. Look out corporate America, smart, motivated and refined women leaders are on the move. Enjoy your journey to the top!

The goals of this book ***are***:

- to empower women to move to the executive suite through transformation.

- to stand with women from a place of love and in service to all women so they can step into their executive greatness.

- to provide women with the hidden, hard hitting facts others are not sharing which are holding them back.

- to share insights with male leaders about the issues women face, to partner and work together more effectively, to understand a woman's perspective and/or cultivate women leaders within their organization.

- to provide women with a place to journal, plan and brainstorm about their 10 Steps to the Top.

This book *is not*:

- about men versus women. It does call out areas where a woman's attributes are not serving her to achieve her professional greatness given the business environment has been designed by men.

- for faint-hearted women but is for those who are serious about refining themselves to amplify their leadership abilities and leave behind those that are limiting them.

- about right or wrong. It is about moving from good to great and great to extraordinary.

- about absolutes. Almost any sentences could begin with "Many have found ..." The spirit and intent of this book is to share insights and perspectives that challenge women to bring their "best selves" to their business and leadership journey.

- about losing yourself or transforming at the expense of who you are. It is about the deep exploration and amplification of your very best attributes and allowing them to shine.

Special Acknowledgments

To my Mother for leading with grace, wisdom, strength and abundant love.

To Jean Otte for publishing *Changing the Corporate Landscape* and to the Women Unlimited team for their partnerships with global corporations and empowering women leaders through their intensive leadership-development programs. I am proud to be an alumna! It was during my year with Women Unlimited when I was inspired to develop this Ten-Step Leadership Development Program.

I would also like to acknowledge Cisco Leaders/Women Unlimited graduates who delivered this program globally to the Cisco Connected Women's Network: Rima Almandine, Lynley Novello, Pamela Autorino, Ellen Lail, Brenda Dennis, Sandy Bologna, Julie Thomas, and Hope Galley. To the women leaders from Cisco who always said "Yes" when we reach out for their sage advice: Wendy Bahr, Patrice D'Eramo, Stephanie Carullo, Luanne Tierney, Rebecca Jacoby and Blair Christie. Thank you for being extraordinary role models and leaders. A special thank you to Jamie Garcia for wanting to create a better workplace for women.

As a member of the International Coaching Federation, I would also like to acknowledge Accomplishment Coaching for broadening my awareness and understanding of "Being" and the power transformation can have professionally and personally. Accomplishment Coaching's philosophy is woven throughout the messages found in this book, and their purpose is captured in their vision, mission and core values statements below.

Vision: The Greatness of Human Beings Unleashed, Power and Possibility for All.

Mission: Setting the worldwide standard of excellence, we lead, coach, and train in the service of transforming lives.

Core Values:

Possibility: Possibility is all that can be. There is possibility beyond what seems reasonable, predictable, comfortable, or attainable.

Responsibility: Being responsible leaves people at the source of their lives, at choice, and able to act effectively.

Integrity & Well-Being: Integrity and well-being are the foundation to having a life or business that works. Fundamental to integrity are completion and authenticity. Fundamental to well-being is self-care.

Essence: People have a pure, essential nature. Operating from this place, people create extraordinary relationships and unprecedented results in their lives.

Love: Love is what exists naturally within and between people. Removing the barriers to the experience of this love profoundly alters the quality of people's lives.

Introduction

FIND YOUR TRUE NORTH

Long before consumer navigational systems were available, I would spend hours looking at maps and kept a compass in my car. As long as I had a compass with me, I never felt lost. One of my innate gifts has always been to map out the most effective route to get to my destination. Did I always take the most direct route to get from point A to point B? Absolutely not! I took many wrong turns and encountered unexpected detours and that was the best part of the journey! Extraordinary experiences await you off the beaten path, when you are detoured or you take a wrong turn. What gives you confidence to adapt when your journey deviates from the original plan? You need to know where "Your True North" is, by knowing yourself, your career goals, and most importantly, your life goals. This clarity acts as your compass and guide so no matter what unexpected detours you may encounter along the way, you can always get back on course.

True North is a constant and refers to the geographic North Pole.

Magnetic north tends to shift and refers to the Earth's magnetic field.

Adjust your magnetic compass to stay aligned with "Your True North."

For business leaders with aspirational goals of leading an organization at the senior executive level, it is not unusual for to them to have a career plan that is mapped out as far out as five years. And while every effort is made to create the fastest, most direct route for your career that far out, in business, all this plan can be is a road map to guide you directionally where you want to go. Most of my career jumps came from a phone call or a request from someone that was not factored into my career plan. Someone knew of my work and was recommending me for a position. Being flexible and adaptable allows you to quickly course-correct and be open to all the possibilities that await you by taking a different route. There are many new things to learn and explore as your life's adventure unfolds—detours, storms, and even a collision or two can occur, so bring your compass and be prepared to make adjustments and you will always find your way back to "Your True North."

ARE YOU READY?

The purpose of this book is to connect with you, woman-to-woman, and provide you with important insights that others are not sharing with you that are vital to your success in business. This is the book I needed to read twenty years ago to avoid the obstacles I encountered and accelerate my professional success. For the busy executive, I have included a one-page survival guide to keep in your daily planner for quick reference. All of the forms referenced within the book can be downloaded for free from my website www.TrueNorthEnterprise.com, by entering the code: "Boardroom" to design and create your abundant and unique.

I have committed my life to empowering girls and women to achieve their dreams. I hope this book provides the road map for more women to reach the senior-executive-level, chief-level, and the boardroom. As we begin, I must caution you that you may not like what you read. You may challenge the premise and want to blame your career barriers on your management, the men in your organization, or the glass ceiling. All of those elements are external to you, and while you have no direct control over the individuals, you do have the ability to influence their judgment and perspective of you in a positive way. In order to do that, you must be willing and have the courage to begin your journey from a place of *brutal honesty with yourself* and make the important changes within your control to get to the top. Are you ready to make that investment in yourself?

If you are happy where you are and your career plans do not include climbing the corporate ladder, you may find many of these suggestions too extreme or determine that it is not worth making the adjustments in your "business way of being," and that is perfectly okay. This book is for those who have declared in their life that they want to be a senior leader or executive and are willing to continually explore the very best of themselves and adjust or leave behind their less-desirable behaviors. You are a diamond in the rough, and every life experience is an investment in who you are meant to become. This book is your guide to polishing the rough edges, developing the perfect facets, and creating your unique leadership style. I hope this book becomes one of the tools you use that allows everyone to see your brilliance, sparkle and appreciate that you are expensive (and worth every penny)!

It's Not a Man-versus-Woman Issue

All great leaders have a similar mission—to create a followership in others and to ignite their potential by aligning them to the broader vision and help them see how each individual has an impact on the bigger picture. What differs are the approaches and techniques used.

Historically, business leaders have been men and they have designed the corporate business model. It's a fact. It is within this construct that women have the opportunity to excel, if they understand how to navigate the environment effectively. It has been an evolutionary journey with women striving to find their way to the top while being true to their authentic-self and successfully adapting to a male dominant business culture. For more than three decades after the women's liberation movement, women still struggle to obtain senior level executive positions. Women work hard, potentially too hard, to demonstrate to male executives that they "have what it takes" to become great business leaders by focusing their energy on learning how to behave like men. In the eighties and nineties, women conditioned themselves to act like men, dress like men, speak like men, and find ways to relate to men.

In the late eighties, I attended a conference where the theme focused on adapting women's communication styles to succeed in business. One of the exercises compared the communication styles of women and men in meetings. One of the examples demonstrated that a woman makes twenty-six gestures when entering the room and getting situated at the table in comparison to a man's seven. Workshops like this were prominent during this window of time, instilling into women the need to create masks that women would wear in business to demonstrate that we were smart, capable and deserved a seat in the boardroom. Women learned how to communicate in business by modifying their style to emulate men. It would take many years for women to find their own authentic business style and for the culture of business to adapt to their unique attributes as women leaders. As a result, more women leaders are now emerging within the highest levels of government and corporate executive roles, and there is still a long way to go. As of July of 2012, there were forty-one female CEO's in the Fortune 1000 (4.1%).[1] A listing of the extraordinary leaders can be found in the Resources section. In addition to thriving in the current business environment, it will be interesting to witness what will change when companies that are *started by women* begin to join the Fortune 1000.

WOMEN HAVE WHAT IT TAKES WITHIN

I am a graduate of Women Unlimited, an intensive, one-year executive-development program, and have clients who are extraordinary women from Fortune 500 companies. All these women are focused on achieving their business greatness and are frustrated with what is stopping them from breaking the perceived "glass ceiling." Much of the frustration women are experiencing is a result of their striving to be their authentic selves while having to filter the information in a way to be best received by their male audience. Women are not adapting effectively enough to make the jump beyond middle management or operations and are left to play a supportive role to the vision or mission because there are elements of their behavior and communication style that carry *too many* female-specific attributes. ***Women are not being given the direct and honest truth so they can make the changes. This may be a result of Human Relations policies, avoiding what could be perceived as a "gender-specific" conversation or they just don't feel like addressing all the emotion that comes with the feedback.*** That is where I come in!

LIGHTENING UP AND BEING LIKEABLE

Women are exhausted. For many their career is a significant part of a very complicated system that includes being a wife, a mother, an extended family member, a care provider, a community member, a teacher, a healer, a psychologist, and the list goes on. Trying to figure it all out, "trying to have it all," leaves women depleted and fatigued. It requires a significant amount of effort, mental energy, and emotional preparation to adapt our innate attributes to participate in the serious game of business. As a result, women who are trying to juggle it all become masterful at time management. Managing every moment of the day becomes crucial to getting it all done. Women have become focused execution machines who have little time for small talk, and the perception is that we are too serious and intense. Women didn't factor into their plan that they also needed to be "likeable."

Another consistent disconnect on getting promoted was women's perception of what is required to get promoted. Women consistently believe that "if I work hard and do a great job, I will be recognized and get promoted." But these are not the rules of the game; women are missing the signals. Dee Dee Myers, White House press secretary to President Clinton, shares in her book *Why Women Should Rule the World*, that "as the first woman to serve as White House Press Secretary, I definitely felt at times trapped by these competing expectations. I was supposed to be authoritative; after all, I was speaking for the President of the United States, The Most Powerful Man on Earth. But at the same time, I had to be likable—a quality that's a bonus, not a requirement, for men in the same position."[2]

Smart, serious, intelligent, driven, organized, and focused women were missing promotion opportunities because in the midst of their hectic day they just didn't have enough time and did not plan in their day the importance of networking, having lunch and lightening up. Women were not getting the hard facts on what would prevent them from moving forward. It's time to correct our course!

WE ARE BETTER TOGETHER

This book was created for the *busy businesswoman* with the understanding that she has little time to invest in herself to bring her best innate skills and authentic spirit to the conversation, empowering her to achieve her personal and professional goals. Until you put down the masks and stop playing the "fake it till you make it" game (how many times have you heard that cliché, ladies?) you will be limited in your ability to achieve the greatness you deserve, and you risk being unhappy even if you achieve it. Why? Because it is not who you authentically are!

The goal of this book is to give women the insight, tools, and permission to truly be their authentic selves and bring their best attributes to the business world. Show your leaders the strong, smart and bold[3] woman executive you are! It's time to create a business environment that allows women to take the masks off and invite men to see that we are smart, capable and likable leaders. Let's shift the conversation to what men and women in business can accomplish together— leveraging our innate skills, our combined talents, and our unique perspectives and creating innovative solutions that look at the opportunity from many different facets of the prism. We are better together!

Are you prepared to be honest with yourself and commit to take the first step (or shall I say ten steps) to begin your transformation into an extraordinary, sought-after, inspirational, and motivational leader? Let's get started!

Step 1: Who Am I and What Do I Want?

Individuals will follow strong leaders who: (1) know who they are, (2) know what they want, (3) know where they are going, and (4) know how to get there.

WHO AM I?

In speaking with many women as an executive and life-transformation coach, I usually begin the conversation with "What do you want?" In almost every instance, women answer, "I'm not sure." As we begin exploring who they are, what they believe their purpose is, what they want to accomplish during their life's journey, what they love to do, and what they loathe doing, they begin to discover who they are and what they want.

This first step is intentional. Before you can ask anyone to help you achieve everything you want in your life, you need to know what you want. Before you can begin to know what you want, it's important to answer the question, "Who am I?"

Far too many women, especially those in the midst of raising children and being a wonderful wife, loving daughter, sister, and supportive friend while being an extraordinary businesswoman, have forgotten to include themselves in the priority list and need to get reacquainted with themselves. So before we can begin, let's explore "Who am I?" and "What do I want?"

Most of this book is focused on the business aspects of who you are and what you want. Before you create the course for your career, let's bring it back to a few fundamental questions about your life. Do you know the answers to these questions about yourself?

1. Who am I?   Yes   No
2. Why am I here?   Yes   No
3. What do I love and want more of in my life?   Yes   No
4. Am I happy with all aspects of my life?   Yes   No

Were you able to answer a resounding "Yes" to all four questions? Clarity around these four questions will lay a strong foundation that supports what you want in your life which will then align with your career plan. So before you can articulate what you want, let's take a moment to explore how you can answer these questions "Yes!" or make the course corrections to lay a strong foundation for what you want.

For those who wish to explore in detail who you are and what your purpose is, there is no shortage of tools to conduct a self-analysis. There are:

1. Myers-Briggs (I am an ENTJ.)[4]
2. StrengthsFinders 2.0 (I am Individualization, Relator, Futuristic, Strategic & Competition)[5]
3. Passion Profile (I am Builder, Transformer, and Altruist.)[6]
4. You! Here's how to get to the nitty-gritty of who you are and why you are here.

Let's go with number 4. I want you to find your favorite quiet place—a beach, a mountaintop, your favorite chair or in your yard. Wherever it is, I want you to find a time where you can go there alone for a least one hour or as long as three hours, uninterrupted. If you like, you may take a notebook and pen but no phones or other distracting devices, with one exception— meditation music is allowed. No other music selections for this exercise please!

As you sit quietly and comfortably, I want you to inhale and exhale deeply ten times. For each inhale and exhale, I want you to say to yourself *Who am I?* As you relax, continue asking yourself this question until your mind quiets and you can only hear the sound of your breath and your internal voice asking this question. Look for answers to come from your heart rather than your mind. Pay attention to any responses you receive. When you feel completely relaxed, you can begin asking yourself any or all of the following questions:

1. Who am I?
2. Why am I here?
3. What is my purpose?
4. What makes me happiest?
5. What should I accomplished while I'm here (on earth)?

In the quiet moments, listen to your internal voice (spirit, essence, heart, soul, core, being, etc.) and you will have a different conversation and outcome than any test you could ever take!

Top Five Messages	Who Am I
1.	
2.	
3.	
4.	
5.	

In speaking with individuals who have received life-threatening news, I've found that they sit quietly and ask these very questions. Many vow to live their life from this place and not based on external influences from that point forward. You have the opportunity to learn from their experiences and begin creating the life you want—now. Do not skip this very important step. This is Your Life's True North, and your personal and professional plans will evolve from here. This clarity will be your compass and always guide you back when life's detours present themselves.

What Do I Want? My Life Priorities

Now that you have more clarity around who you are and why you are here, let's explore what you want to achieve in life by creating your "Life Priorities Map," which will bring into focus (1) what you love in your life and would like to have more of and (2) what you loathe in your life and would like to have less of. The obvious goal is to increase what you love in your life and reduce what you don't. As obvious as it may seem, many people are not living their lives from a place that brings them happiness, joy, and fulfillment. This is especially true in their professional life.

Life Priorities Map	
Things I Love	**Things I Loathe**
1.	1.
2.	2.
3.	3.
4.	4.
5.	5.
6.	6.
7.	7.
8.	8.
9.	9.
10.	10.

Having completed the Who Am I and My Life Priorities exercises, do you have a clearer picture of who you are and what you would like to see more of in your professional and personal life? Do you also see what you would like less of in your life? Do you see any patterns?

A successful IT consulting CEO shared with me that she just did not feel happy or satisfied, even though everything she touched turned to gold. After exploring what she loved to do and what she did not enjoy doing, a pattern emerged: she loved children, she loved to write, and she loved to teach (in addition to being an executive). By looking at her life from a place of unlimited potential and unencumbered discovery about what gave her the most happiness, she has added writing children's books to her life's journey. This exercise allowed her to see her life holistically and blend her life priorities together creating an integrated life. Having clarity around who she is, what her life purpose and innate talents are, she could define what "having it all meant," based on her priorities and life aspirations. She no longer sees her life in siloed compartments but rather as "what she does" is an expression of "who she is" in all facets of her life. While this book is predominantly about business, you will read in Step 4: Put Yourself First; Not Last that you live an integrated life. As a result, you need to factor in how all the decisions you make in your business life affect your personal life and vice versa. Align the priorities in your life holistically *first,* and secondarily align your professional goals. Once you determine who you are and what you want in your integrated life, you will have more clarity and confidence to ask for what you need.

MY NAVIGATIONAL ROAD MAPS

Sharing what you want in your life creates an environment for others to support you and cheer you on both professionally and in your personal life. You have a fan club of family and friends who want to see you be successful. They want to see you live your dreams. You are not alone, so create an abundant life filled with endless possibilities! One of the tools you can use to capture very specific, measurable goals in support of being a great leader with an integrated life plan is the "Life Navigational Road Maps." You will notice that it begins with "self" followed by what you want in your relationships, career, and lifestyle. Create as many goals as you would like and explore all aspects of your life to create a wonderful, integrated personal and professional life with the support you need to achieve it! (These plans are in addition to your business plans, which should always be current and in alignment with your company, department and team's goals.)

WHAT DO YOU WANT? YOUR LIFE NAVIGATIONAL ROAD MAPS

Self:	Specific Details of Your Aspirational Goals	Resources: People & Tools	Due Date
1.			
2.			
3.			
4.			
5.			

Relationships:	Specific Details of Your Aspirational Goals	Resources: People & Tools	Due Date
1.			
2.			
3.			
4.			
5.			

Career:	Specific Details of Your Aspirational Goals	Resources: People & Tools	Due Date
1.			
2.			
3.			
4.			
5.			

Lifestyle:	Specific Details of Your Aspirational Goals	Resources: People & Tools	Due Date
1.			
2.			
3.			
4.			
5.			

With more clarity around who you are, your life priorities and plans to achieve your aspirational goals with resources and a timeline, it is important to socialize your plans so others know what you would like to achieve and their role to help you achieve it.

HOW TO ASK FOR WHAT YOU WANT

When asking for what you want in any of the categories above and especially in business, which is our focus, it is important to enroll the individual and their involvement in your success. It is helpful to create a story that helps them visualize what success looks like by sponsoring you for what you want. Do not take shortcuts in preparing for the meeting. If possible, be sure to articulate what is in it for them. Create a summary or bulleted list of topics that support the conversation flow, taking them on a journey so they can see the value in partnering with you to get what you want.

Let's use asking for a raise as an example. It's 2012 and there is a 23 percent disparity in salary between men and women doing the same jobs. That's $23 out of every $100 that women are missing—that's a lot of income you are not receiving over the course of your career! You can do the math on what this means to you personally and to your family. Given its importance, it is worth advocating for yourself to get a raise!

1. Do your homework and then prepare a compelling position as to why you deserve a raise. A few areas to consider:
   a. revenue you have generated for the company
   b. customer testimonials in support of your work
   c. saving the company money
   d. increasing operational efficiencies for the company

2. Shift from focusing on what you "need" to what you "deserve." If possible, research the salary potential for your position prior to the negotiation.

3. Ask for more than you believe you deserve and position your value and why you deserve it. It's a negotiation; so go a little higher in anticipation of give and take.

4. Focus only on the positives and what the possibility looks like in the future with you in the role.

5. Do not give ultimatums, but be prepared to leave the role or company if you feel you are being treated unfairly, and be confident in your ability to get the income you deserve.

Another example is negotiating your title. Don't let anyone tell you that the title doesn't matter! While there may be differences between a vice president in a large company and the vice president of a small company, the title of vice president holds merit and credibility. Large organizations tend to limit the number of executive titles offered, as there are perks, incentives, and approvals associated with these positions. There is a fascinating psychological dynamic that occurs in large organizations where first- and second-level managers are generating hundreds of millions of dollars of revenue for the company, and yet they are limited to the title of manager or director. These managers and directors are equivalent to the CEO of a smaller company, and yet their title is limiting. For these individuals, their title keeps them trapped when they want to jump to another organization. It is difficult to jump to a vice-president-level position from a manager title even if you have extensive qualifications. The title creates the perception that they are not a player. It may not be true, but that is the perception. Negotiating your title establishes a degree of credibility and status and provides you with access to individuals of similar credentials. There will be times when you'll jump for salary, and there'll be times you'll jump for title. Do not let anyone make you feel ashamed that you want the title. Establish the reasons why you deserve it and negotiate it.

Enrolling others into your success requires you to know what you want and articulate their role in helping you achieve it. Focus on the business outcomes and opportunity that will be generated, and share your professional aspirations and your personal life goals with others. Ask them for their feedback, mentorship, and most importantly, sponsorship to ensure your success. Always be prepared to ask for what you want, and be prepared to course-correct when unexpected roadblocks occur. Every detour presents you with another opportunity to ask yourself, *What do I want?* and create the plan to go get it!

Act Decisively

On your journey, you will be placed in many situations where important decisions need to be made. Women tend to overanalyze the situation and data before making decisions. This slows women down and blocks them from getting what they want in business, their career goals and in their personal life.

The founder of Women Unlimited, Jean Otte, shared during one of her leadership sessions that when she interviews senior executives of corporations, they share that the most important area of development needed for women to join the senior leadership team is to be more decisive in their decision making and have confidence in their decision-making skills.[7] General Colin Powell's formula for decision making is: "Part I: Use the formula P=40 to 70, where P stands for the probability of success and the numbers indicate the percentage of information acquired. Part II: Once the information is in the 40 to 70 range, go with your gut."[8]

Many women share that their strategy has been to gather as much data as possible and conduct a thorough and complete analysis before making a recommendation or asking for what they want. As I explore why this is a consistent pattern with women, many look back to their early days of education and their desire to get the "A" and receive acknowledgement and recognition for doing a great job. Pavlovian behavior instilled in them that if they worked hard and studied more, they would be successful. Those skills, which served girls well in their educational journey, would prove to be a barrier to women and their success in business. At the root cause of this "analysis paralysis" is fear. Many women use the analysis of data as a shield, protecting them from questions they may receive from other leaders or their peers. Women over prepare to address their fear of not having an answer to a question they might receive. Women invest a great deal of time and energy overanalyzing data to proactively prepare for anything that may come their way.

Women find it uncomfortable to be responsible for an initiative or project and not be prepared to get an "A." This learned behavior is holding women back. Women need to get comfortable with not having all the answers to every question. When you need to buy some time, you can graciously respond with "That is a good question. Let me reflect on that or investigate that and I'll follow up with you." This response demonstrates business confidence and removes the fear of failure or fear of judgment. Ultimately, women who try too hard to have all the answers by studying all the data project their fear to their audience and leaders, and it shows. Unfortunately, this adds time to the project, increases your stress level, and sets you up for disappointment when the receiver does not value the extra effort you put in to the project. This often results in a feeling of being unappreciated and without the recognition you had hoped for a job well done. This is a consistent challenge for women, and it is holding them back. Going forward, take the time to speak with your leaders about what they require in the final deliverable and provide that to them. Don't overdo it. If they do not want or need it, you are not going to get acknowledged for it, and it's creating more work for you, do not do it! By having a conversation with them and creating a deliverable based on what they need, you will get back valuable time and have less stress in your life. Make sure you understand the priority of the project and the deliverable that is expected. This will create alignment between you and your leadership, so resist the temptation to get an "A" if it's not required for this deliverable!

In the current fast-paced speed of global business, waiting too long to make a decision in the senior ranks is detrimental to the viability and growth of today's largest corporations. Today's leaders are expected to leverage their teams, gather the data, ask critical questions, and make an informed decision with approximately 40 percent to 70 percent of the data. It requires courage; it requires an educated degree of risk taking and the ability to adapt quickly with a contingent plan. In order to articulate what you want, gather the data without over analysis and make the request from a confident place knowing that you always have a contingency plan. Successful leaders who make it to the top possess the ability to gather an appropriate amount of data and make a decision.

An aspect of this over analysis is that women get mentally and emotionally invested in the information. It prevents women from having an open mind to other perspectives, suggestions, or comments because they done all the analysis. So when the question is posed or an idea is shared, it triggers something internally at an emotional level. The need to be perfect and get that "A" shows up and triggers our emotions. And this is what becomes visible at a micro-inequity level and sometimes not so subtly. How can women change these learned behaviors? What if you had permission not to get in "A"? What if you gave yourself permission not to over analyze the data and believe in your ability to be a critical thinker and ask great questions to reach a decision? Can you give yourself permission to focus on the business outcomes and make recommendations based on achieving those goals? If you can let go of the fear and trust in yourself and your abilities, people will witness a smart, capable, relaxed, businesswoman who can articulate what she wants. (See also Step 5: Leadership.)

NAVIGATING STEP 1: WHO AM I AND WHAT DO I WANT?

MY JOURNEY TO THE TOP — GUIDE:

- Complete the Who Am I Exercise
- Complete the Life Priorities and Life Navigational Road Map exercises. Include your Business Plan.
- Socialize your ideas. Enroll others.
- Ask for what you want, why you want it, and what support you need to achieve it.
- Make decisions with 40 percent to 70 percent of the information without emotion.
- Gather the facts and act decisively. Focus on the business outcomes, think critically, and take educated risks.

MY JOURNEY TO THE TOP — NOTES:

- ☐ _____
- ☐ _____
- ☐ _____
- ☐ _____
- ☐ _____

MY JOURNEY TO THE TOP — ACTION ITEMS:

- ☐ _____
- ☐ _____
- ☐ _____
- ☐ _____
- ☐ _____

Step 2: Know Your Value to Your Leaders

It's not what you know, but "who knows that you know what you know?"[9] Can you articulate your value to an executive without hesitation when the opportunity presents itself?

Impact You Are Having on Business Results

One of the common misconceptions with women is that if they work hard, they will be recognized and will get the promotion. Unfortunately, this is only a partial truth. While your knowledge of your industry and work performance may be extraordinary, your leaders may not know the value you are bringing in support of helping them exceed their business objectives; they may not realize what you truly know and your value to them, to the business, and most importantly to the customers. This is one of the more uncomfortable topics I discuss with my clients. Women really struggle with promoting themselves. In women's minds it is not humble and comes across as boastful. Women feel like they are bragging. Their entire life many have been told that this was just not a way "young ladies" behave. However we may have learned this behavior, it's time for that to change! If you create a shift in your mindset that "sharing what you know" is not bragging to "I am sharing how I am supporting my leader's success," I think you would agree that it is a radically different message. Letting them know where you are making an impact brings tremendous value to them, and your leaders will know you stand shoulder to shoulder with them, aligned and clear on the mission that lies ahead.

Be a WingWoman

One of the techniques I recommend women use is to have a wingwoman and be a wingwoman (derived from the term, "wingman—the pilot who positions his aircraft outside and behind the wing of the leader of a flying formation"[10]). Find opportunities to acknowledge women during meetings, promote her great work with other leaders, and amplify her message about a project or initiative that is strategic to the team or leader. Ask another woman to do the same for you. This can also be accomplished by writing a thank-you e-mail note to another woman's manager acknowledging her work and copying other leaders. It's an excellent way for women to support women and help them get the recognition they deserve. It's also nice to know that a wingwoman "has your back!" You should also do this in your relationships with men in business—be their wingwoman and ask them to be your wingman! This topic focuses on women promoting women to address their discomfort with self-promotion and acknowledging other women. Men seem to acknowledge each other more naturally and women need to become more comfortable with this business practice.

HAVE YOUR COMMERCIAL READY

Your journey to continue to step into leadership greatness requires that you always know the impact you're having on business results. I cannot emphasize enough the strategic importance to your success to "have your commercial ready" and be able to calmly and succinctly articulate what you've done for them lately at all times. Equally as important is looking over the horizon. Senior leaders are continually looking for individuals they can trust, who support their vision and know how to enroll others for success. Business is not static. It is a dynamically changing environment based on customer demand, market conditions, shareholder value, profitability, and many other factors. Leaders need to know they have access to individuals who can solve complex problems and begin sentences by asking "What if …" or "What opportunity does it create if …" or "What could be possible if …" Always know what your leader's goals are and ensure your projects and efforts are directly aligned. If you are working on something that is not in direct alignment, you need to ask yourself "why?" This focused alignment creates the opportunity for you to continually demonstrate your value to your leaders.

BRING VALUE IN FUTURE ROLES

Share with your leaders how your vision of what's over the horizon has an impact on growth, revenue, and customer concerns, laying the foundation for the position you'd like to create for yourself. Look for opportunities to identify gaps in the business model, problems you can solve, or new trends in the market and develop a business plan in support of creating a new position for yourself within the organization. If a position already exists, share how you can bring innovation to the role and provide new ways to address the future needs of the business.

THE UNDESIRABLE POSITION

There are differing points of view when it comes to taking an undesirable assignment. There are those who believe if it's not in direct support of your Life Navigational Road Map you should not take the assignment. On the other hand, there are those who believe that taking an assignment that others don't want can give you an opportunity to shine. My recommendation is to take the position if the following conditions exist:

1. It is a visible initiative and provides you with access to senior management.
2. It provides advancement within twelve to eighteen months.
3. It is strategic to the organization.
4. It is a struggling organization, and your leadership will absolutely demonstrate an improvement in results.
5. You leverage the role to achieve your long-term career goals after the assignment ends.

Be sure to clarify with your leadership in advance what benefit you will receive by stepping into this role and turning things around. For example, if at the end of twelve months, an increase in revenue of 15 percent is realized, you will receive a bonus or increase in salary. Another area to negotiate would be a new title (i.e., an in-line promotion). Do not take a position only because it is open, you feel forced, you are doing it solely to please someone else or to accommodate a leaders request. You have to see it as a win for you or a major stepping-stone towards what you want to achieve in your career.

KNOWLEDGE IS IN DEMAND. WHAT ARE YOU READING?

Unfortunately, far too many magazines bombard women as we check out at the supermarket deliver messaging that there's something broken that women need to fix. There's nothing wrong with us. There's nothing that needs to be fixed. As we go from good to great and from great to extraordinary, there's always opportunity to accentuate our best features. Avoid the negative messages in these magazines! I encourage you to find books, magazines, and other sources of positive messaging that support your personal vision and business goals. Stop watching reality television unless the show is geared toward developing a passion or skill of yours, like cooking or home design. Fill your life with activities that benefit you, your dreams, your wishes, and your desires and stop watching someone else's life on television—go live yours!

From a business perspective, read everything you can that aligns with your industry. Read what your customers are reading as well as what your leaders are reading. Stay on top of what your competitors are doing and saying and always be prepared with a counter message in support of your company's value to the customer. Leaders are always learning and looking for trends that will make a difference in their business strategy. A few publications that are read by leaders fairly consistently across all industries are the *Harvard Business Review*, the *Economist, Fast Company, Wired,* and the *Wall Street Journal*. Add these and other broad business thought leadership publications to your regular reading. I have included a list of my favorite leadership, business and transformational books in the "Leadership Library" in the Resource section

NAVIGATING STEP 2: KNOW YOUR VALUE TO YOUR LEADERS

MY JOURNEY TO THE TOP — GUIDE:

- Share the Impact you are having on Business Results.

- Be a WingWoman. Have WingWomen and WingMen.

- Always have your Commercial Ready.

- Bring Value in Future Roles. Design your Next Position.

- Knowledge is in Demand. Leaders are Out Front, See Trends and are always Learning.

MY JOURNEY TO THE TOP — NOTES:

☐ _____

☐ _____

☐ _____

☐ _____

☐ _____

MY JOURNEY TO THE TOP — ACTION ITEMS:

☐ _____

☐ _____

☐ _____

☐ _____

☐ _____

Step 3: Executive Presence — What Message Are You Sending?

It has been estimated that leadership presence determines approximately 70 percent of hiring and advancement decisions at senior-management levels, and for women that number can jump to 85 percent.[11] What is your brand and how does it convey your executive presence?

APPEARANCE: INTELLIGENT. ALL BUSINESS

Today's beautiful fashions make it hard for women to consistently represent executive presence. The beautiful shoes, large accessories, form-fitting tops, dresses and suits that reveal too many curves are not serving women well. Don't get me wrong—I love today's fashions, but I recommend that women reserve them for evenings, weekends, women networking events and personal occasions. The two outfits shown here are both very nice. One represents a more formal business suit and the other is an acceptable business dress—or is it? There is nothing provocative about this dress; however, it could be what keeps you from getting a senior-level position.

MEN HAVE FOUR CATEGORIES OF BUSINESS ATTIRE:

1. Business dress (suit and tie)
2. Casual executive (dress slacks, jacket, and open-collared shirt)
3. Business casual (khaki-like slacks with a button-down or golf shirt)
4. Casual (jeans)

How does your wardrobe categories align? I encourage you to take time and review what is in your closet and donate items that are not supporting your executive brand. Two organizations that support women who need business suits are DressForSuccess.org and TheWomensAlliance.org. They would welcome any gently used suits that no longer serve you.

It is fairly predictable that when you are in a business meeting with clients and other executives the attire will be business dress. While not the most exciting attire, women should align with what others are wearing and wear a professional business suit. It could have a skirt or pants—either is fine. Here are a few other recommendations to take your brand to the executive suite.

1. Hairstyle: Select and style your hair so you do not have to touch it or shake your head to get it off your face. It is distracting and a credibility killer.
2. Nails: Keep them short, filed and if you wear polish, choose clear or a light color. If your nails make contact with you keyboard or table surface, you should consider trimming them back.
3. Bare legs: Wear pantyhose or socks to cover any exposed areas of your legs—even during the summer months. It creates a polished look.
4. Shoes: Choose comfortable, non-distracting shoes you can walk in. A classic pump is always a good choice. Do not wear platform shoes, sandals, or open-toe shoes, and avoid "toe cleavage."
5. Perfume: Do not wear perfume to the office or meetings.
6. Handbags: Choose a handbag that makes it easy to find things. Avoid handbags where you have to dig around to find what you need.

When you enter a room, your pen and business card and notebook should be easily accessible without creating a distraction.

7. Jewelry: Consider limiting the amount of jewelry to seven pieces: two rings, a necklace, a watch, one pair of non-dangling earrings, a bracelet, and perhaps a lapel pin. The jewelry worn should not make noise and should not be distracting. Accessories are an important part of creating your executive image. Have fun selecting what represents your brand while keeping the attention on your business capabilities.

8. Dresses and skirts: Try to get the hemline to touch the knee to allow two inches of "ride-up" allowance. Anything higher can reveal too much.

9. Pants: Slacks should fall away from the body at the midpoint of the derriere and should not conform to your shape beyond that point. Wear a blazer, jacket or sweater if the slacks are too revealing.

10. Blouses and shirts: The blouse should fit so there is no evidence of cleavage and should not pucker when you move.

11. Undergarments: The right undergarments provide the foundation needed to present a polished, finished package. Invest in undergarments that support your business attire and create a refined executive look:
    a. Bras: Wear full-coverage bras. If needed, go for a fitting with a professional.
    b. Underpants: Wear the appropriate undergarments so you do not have panty lines. Buy a full-length mirror and be sure to check the view from behind. There are always people behind you, so pay attention to what message you are sending when you walk away.
    c. Slips and Camisoles: There are so many types to choose from today—traditional, loose-fitting, or those that slim. Wear a slip or camisole when the outfit has any transparency or you need to create a layer to prevent revealing the outline of your body when you walk or when in the wind. If you are wearing a camisole under a shirt or blouse, no lace should be exposed.
    d. At no time should your undergarments be visible.

Do not let your appearance be the reason you did not get the promotion.

Consider hiring an image consultant or fashion stylist to select the best clothes for your body type. Department stores provide this service as well as make-up consultations. Review magazines and use the Internet to find hairstyles worn by women leaders and consult with your hair stylist to select the right style for your face shape and hair type. Another area to consider is to have a few suits custom made. There are tailors in every city that provide this service, and it's wonderful to select the fabric and know that the suit is going to fit you perfectly. Investing in your appearance is one of the best investments you can make. When you dress for the role you want and couple that with your experience and intellect, you increase the odds to moving into the executive suite. Using these guidelines, your brand demonstrates that you are ready to play in the big leagues and have moved past the latest fashion trends and understand the uniform of business. It's about trust, intelligence, and business outcomes, not what's on the runway!

Voice: Strong, Confident and Authoritative

This is perhaps the most consistent feedback about women's communication style that is keeping women from moving up the ladder of success. The tone, pitch, and inflection of your voice have a huge impact on how your brand and presence are interpreted. Leaders share that it is torture to listen to women who have not learned to speak with a professional voice by speaking from their diaphragm. The diaphragm is a set of muscles at the base of your rib cage, below your lungs and above your abdomen. Confident leaders speak from their diaphragm. You can locate it by touching the base of your rib cage and practice inhaling deeply. Take several deep breaths expanding from your diaphragm. This will take some practice as we are naturally inclined to take shallow breaths from our upper chest and lungs. Practice reading books and magazines out loud as you make this a natural part of your speaking voice. Speaking from your diaphragm creates projection, strength, and confidence, which are vital to executive presence.

When attending a meeting with many individuals in the room, project your voice to the furthest person in the room and not only to the person to whom you are directing your response. When women participate in a meeting in a large room, their voices tend to become quiet and soften when responding to a direct question. There is a natural inclination to make that one-on-one connection. In a large group it is important to direct your response for the entire room to hear and not only to the individual to whom you are speaking. For women, it damages your executive presence when you are continually asked to speak up.

I have included information from the Body Language University's website about how the vocal cords work so you can understand what the vocal cords are doing and that when you are nervous or excited your pitch gets even higher.

> *Women tend to have higher voices because they have shorter vocal cords. The length and thickness of the vocal cords, however, are not the only factors that affect one's pitch. The pitch of someone's voice can also be affected by emotions, moods and inflection. Interestingly, our emotions can also affect the pitch of our voices. When people become frightened or excited, the muscles around the voice box (or larynx) unconsciously contract, putting strain on the vocal cords, making the pitch higher.*[2]

Women have a tendency to speak quickly while presenting their ideas or fielding questions from other leaders when stressed. Their inflection and pitch increase, which hurts their executive presence. The receiver interprets this as fear, weakness and a lack of confidence. Here are a few techniques and examples you can use that allow you to deliver your message from a place of power and confidence while addressing the business issue. (Also use this technique for Step 7: Understanding and Managing Conflict) Practice this until it is a natural part of your executive style.

TECHNIQUE:

1. Use silence to create an intentional pause. This is very powerful and increases your executive presence.
2. Take a breath from your diaphragm, and more importantly, *exhale* fully. This gives you time to reflect on your response. It also increases the oxygen into your body, which reduces stress and allows you to think clearly.
3. Deliver a solution-focused response. Do not tell a story.
4. Close with a question requesting alignment, support, or consensus.

EXAMPLE 1:

As we look for innovative solutions to increase revenue this year, I propose that we implement an online ordering solution and promote our product via the latest social networking sites. Is everyone in agreement with this approach?

EXAMPLE 2:

While the product marketing campaign did not achieve the desired results, we have greater clarity into the market and can adapt the campaign based on our findings. We can re-launch the campaign within the next two weeks. Would that be acceptable to everyone?

EXAMPLE 3:

The team has spent a significant amount of time looking at workflow optimization to drive inefficiencies out of our processes and increase profitability. I believe we can save the company $100,000 over the next twelve months by automating several of our manual steps. Can you nominate someone to represent your organization on the task force?

SOCIALIZING: YOUR BRAND AT EVENTS

One of the more delicate areas for women in business is how their brand is represented during social events. There will be opportunities for you to attend corporate functions, dinners with clients, or networking events. Here are a few sage tips to ensure that your brand shines when you are outside of the office environment:

1. Do not drink alcohol—period. One of the techniques used by senior leaders is to order beverages like club soda with lemon, cranberry and seltzer, or a cola with a lime wedge. No one needs to know that you are not consuming alcohol. Using this strategy allows you to keep your head clear and focused on what you want to achieve at the event. The advice I give my clients is to ensure that you mingle and interact with everyone you can, leaving a positive impression. You do not want to be the topic of office conversation the next day due to a lapse

in judgment or being the life of the party. By not drinking alcohol, your thoughts are clear, your energy remains high, and you will be able to perform the next day. When you are in social settings, participate in engaging conversations, bring a sense of humor and lightheartedness to those you meet. Have fun at the event, but leave alcohol out of the equation.

In the United States blood alcohol absorption of greater than .08 is over the legal limit. You would be arrested for a DUI and taken to jail. The consequences are intentionally harsh. Do not drink and drive. A DUI could cost you your job and your ability to be hired and make your life extremely difficult. While drinking may be socially acceptable, it has no positive benefits for your career, your well-being, or your life. There is a huge cost associated with this social practice, and for women on their way to the top, remove it from all aspect of your business engagements! For women who travel internationally, most countries have a legal drinking limit of 0.05 percent. The United States, Canada, Mexico, and the United Kingdom are the most lenient at 0.08 percent.

2. Another delicate aspect to managing your brand during a social event is how to gracefully extract yourself from an uncomfortable situation and keep your brand and relationships intact. This could be a heated conversation, an encounter that is consuming too much time, being caught with someone who has had too much to drink, or improper advances being made. I recommend that women have a few canned responses either when entering the conversation or extracting yourself to ensure that it is not negatively interpreted. A few examples follow:

    a. When entering a conversation where you only can afford a brief visit, begin by letting them know that it is great to see them and you only have a minute or two but wanted to make sure you stopped by to say hello.

    b. In some work environments, women actually come together as a support and rescue team to extract a colleague from encounters. Before joining the group, let one your wingwomen know to interrupt you at a specific time interval or based on an agreed-upon signal.

    c.   When you need to get yourself out of any conversation, state that you have another commitment, meeting, or engagement that requires your attention. Close with how great it was to see them.

Creating and practicing a few "go-to" responses that you can call upon to gracefully exit a conversation or situation is beneficial and prevents the need for you to create something on the fly.

3.   If you need to meet with clients or colleagues outside of an office setting, propose that you have coffee or lunch. Try to avoid extending an invitation for cocktails or dinner. This strategy eliminates any possible confusion and sends the message that you are all business. This can sometimes be a limitation for women in business as it is appropriate for our male colleagues to take a male client to dinner. (Men need to determine if dinner is the appropriate venue when their client or colleague is a woman.) If dinner is the only time to get together, see if you can invite others so it is not a one-on-one meeting (which may make your client feel uncomfortable as well). Another approach may be to ask the client what they prefer and prepare accordingly. For example, many men enjoy dinner at a great steakhouse. In making the arrangements, ask them if there is anyone else they would like to attend and, if possible, try to have one of your colleagues attend. If dinner is just the two of you, select an end time and let them know at the beginning of the meal that you need to leave to attend to another commitment. This creates a business environment that allows you to enjoy a wonderful meal, discuss business, and gracefully wrap things up. Of course, no alcohol here either! If needed, step away and let the server know that no matter what cocktail you order, they should not include alcohol. For example, if you order a margarita, they will bring a non-alcoholic margarita.

Your Brand On-Line & Social Media

Leaders are more vulnerable than ever before. They are expected to leverage social networking tools and guide opinion broadly through these mediums. Consider your messaging carefully before you post anything to a blog, Twitter, Facebook, LinkedIn, or other social networking site. The great news is that you're playing on an international stage. Be aware and prepared for the criticisms, comments, and feedback as well as accolades you will receive when you share your opinion.

Today video is everywhere, and individuals are capturing it and sharing it with the world. One posting where you are tagged on a social networking site can be a career killer. The saying used to be "Don't do anything you wouldn't want to appear on the front page of the *Wall Street Journal*." Now the saying is "Don't do anything that can live forever on the Internet."

As with everything in this book, you have a choice. You decide what recommendations will work for you. The intention is to create awareness for women around these topics and a few ideas on how to address them. When making your choices, understand there is very little tolerance in corporate America, in today's litigious society, to promote leaders who do not understand how to present themselves and the corporate brand in a positive way at all times. This advice is provided to empower you to make it to the top and not have any missteps along the way.

Personal Communications: Engaging, Light and Connected

With their complicated and hectic schedules, women have develop creative techniques to engage in relevant conversations with their male clients and colleagues by watching news highlights, skimming the *Wall Street Journal* business listings, or grabbing the sports page and reviewing the highlights. Wise women understand not to make any misrepresentations about the extent of her knowledge because a woman's integrity and reputation are vital in developing her business relationships. Getting caught making misrepresentations about something as casual as a sporting event could be what gets you kicked out of the male club that is based on trust.[13] Connecting with other women differs and could be a quick hug and a "hello, how's the family, love your shoes, and where did you get that suit?" The woman-to-woman connection is radically different than the woman-to-man connection. Take time to engage in conversations by being present with them. Don't fake it! Ask about what is happening in their life and get them to bring you up to speed with what they have been up to since you saw them last.

Unfortunately, in the quest to be acknowledged and recognized as smart, capable, and worthy business colleagues, busy women with little time to socialize became way too serious in business. This resulted from the limited amount of time women had available. Women didn't have time for small talk. Isn't that ironic! When it comes to business, women can be as serious as a heart attack. Unfortunately, for the individual on the receiving end, women's serious, hard-hitting, fact-laden, "I am right" conversations do not leave them with a "likable" impression, and they dread the next encounter. Practice lightening-up your conversation topics. Let go of the need to be right. In casual business conversations, do not discuss business until someone else brings it up first. These tips will also benefit your personal relationships outside the office. Explore what the conversation might be like where you are not driving an agenda topic or specific outcome. To support your transformation to show that you are "likeable" and draw people towards you, Maya Angelou captures the sentiment beautifully: "I've learned that people will forget what you said, people will forget what you did, but people will never forget how you made them feel."[14] So practice leaving people feeling great about you, the conversation, and the relationship.

Business Impact: Insightful Questions, Confident Statements

An approach that is impactful to establish your executive presence is to ask insightful questions. Reporters do this to extract information to tell the story. As leaders we can learn from the techniques used by reporters who seek to answer these baseline categories of questions: who, what, where, when, why, and how. Be sure these questions are answered when you look at any business issue. A few other insightful questioning techniques business leaders use include the following:

- How does this compare and contrast with prior years or other initiatives?

- What is the impact to the customer, profitability, shareholder value, and other business parameters?

- Does this align with our vision, mission, and core values?

- Do we need to address this internally or should it be outsourced?

- What if we did nothing?

- Does anyone else need to be involved?

- What is the impact to our resources (people, systems and finances)?

Managing Emotion

This is touched on throughout the book, but is worth mentioning as a part of your executive presence — the importance of managing your emotions. Anger, fear, sadness, disgust, surprise, anticipation, trust, and joy are the eight basic categories of emotion.[15] Executives are self-aware and understand when these show up. Rising women leaders need to recognize these emotions and learn to separate them from the business data. Women leaders who express these emotions subtly or boldly get labeled as "emotional." This does not mean that as an executive woman you don't have emotion; on the contrary — the best leaders have emotion, but do not allow their emotions to effect the business discussion and outcomes. They are masterful at focusing on the issue and leveraging their intellect to guide the decision making process. These are the women who are breaking through the glass ceiling in corporate America and achieving leadership positions within government.

Executive presence extends far beyond your appearance. In addition to being smart and knowledgeable about your business area, take time to refine the attributes within you and within your control to increase the probability of getting promoted.

<u>Navigating Step 3: Executive Presence — What Message Are You Sending?</u>

<u>My Journey to the Top — Guide:</u>

- Appearance: Intelligent. All Business.

- Voice: Strong, Confident, and Authoritative.

- Socializing: Protect your Brand at Events and with Clients/ Colleagues

- Social Media: Leverage it wisely to maximize your Presence.

- Communications Personal: Engaging, Light, Connected Conversations. Be "Likeable."

- Communications Business: Insightful Questions, Confident Statements as Leader.

- Manage your Emotions: Know when they show up and focus on the data to make decisions.

<u>My Journey to the Top — Notes:</u>

- ☐ _____
- ☐ _____
- ☐ _____
- ☐ _____
- ☐ _____

<u>My Journey to the Top — Action Items:</u>

- ☐ _____
- ☐ _____
- ☐ _____
- ☐ _____
- ☐ _____

Step 4: Put Yourself First; Not Last

Leaders understand the importance of balance in their lives. Make it a priority to attend to your personal goals, dreams, and plans each day. You will realize greater balance and increased satisfaction in your personal life and professional career.

YOUR WELL-BEING. REINVENTING YOURSELF

For years the term "work-life balance" was used to try to describe how women could "balance" their lives. This made it seem that women were compartmentalized and needed to balance the various areas of their lives. It created an environment where women were present in the business world during certain hours of the day and then threw a switch inside that shifted them to the personal aspects of their lives. That may have worked before the age of mobility.

In today's continually connected, mobile world, information is available to us literally at the tip of our fingers. The new reality is labeled "an integrated life," which means that you work 24x7 and you play 24x7. If managed correctly, mobility is a beautiful thing. It allows you to set your priorities into the framework of your hectic life. If your employer supports it, mobility gives you choices of when, where, and how you get the work done and doesn't necessarily mean you are limited by the time constructs of the nine-to-five job. The beauty of this model is that you can "have it all" based on the life you want to design. The risk many career-oriented women face is managing how much of her time is given to work. This creates a wonderful opportunity to explore how you want to align your time in support of the holistic life you want to create that incorporates and balances your career. The graphical pyramids below represent what many women depict is the reality of their "work-life balance."

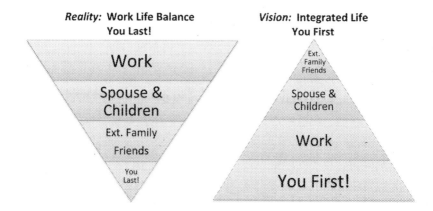

Look at how precarious the pyramid is on the left; so much is resting on "You." Isn't it ironic that if everything is dependent upon you, your well-being is the smallest part of the pyramid? From a well-being perspective, the pyramid on the right makes much more sense. From this place, you have so much more to give to others and everyone benefits! The question becomes how to create an integrated life with all the demands and complexities and, most importantly, place yourself first and not last when there are only twenty-four hours in a day!

DESIGN THE IDEAL DAY

The ideal day—does it exist? How can I create it based on my Integrated Life Map? Ellen Lail, VP of Sales for VCE, Inc., shared a colorful way of looking at her day. By color-coding your activities (using categories in your calendaring software or highlighters) — for example, pink for well-being, purple for family time, blue for work activities, and yellow for travel time—it becomes clear "where did the day go?"

The example that follows represents the perfect fictitious workday. It starts at five o'clock in the morning and places priority on health and well-being. It then allows for travel time to the office and a full eight-hour workday to meet our employer's expectations. It includes lunch, enough time to travel home from work, prepare a meal for the family, and spend quality time with them before bedtime, and leaves enough time to squeeze in evening grooming to get to bed by ten o'clock for a full night's rest. Whew!

Today	"My Perfect Fictious Day"
5:00	Health & Well-Being Time (Pink)
5:30	Health & Well-Being Time (Pink)
6:00	Grooming (Pink)
6:30	Grooming (Pink)
7:00	Breakfast & Family Time (Purple)
7:30	Breakfast & Family Time (Purple)
8:00	Travel Time (Yellow)
8:30	Office Projects, Meetings and Planning (Blue)
9:00	Office Projects, Meetings and Planning (Blue)
9:30	Office Projects, Meetings and Planning (Blue)
10:00	Office Projects, Meetings and Planning (Blue)
10:30	Office Projects, Meetings and Planning (Blue)
11:00	Office Projects, Meetings and Planning (Blue)
11:30	Office Projects, Meetings and Planning (Blue)
12:00	Lunch (Pink)
12:30	Lunch (Pink)
1:00	Office Projects, Meetings and Planning (Blue)
1:30	Office Projects, Meetings and Planning (Blue)
2:00	Office Projects, Meetings and Planning (Blue)
2:30	Office Projects, Meetings and Planning (Blue)
3:00	Office Projects, Meetings and Planning (Blue)
3:30	Office Projects, Meetings and Planning (Blue)
4:00	Office Projects, Meetings and Planning (Blue)
4:30	Office Projects, Meetings and Planning (Blue)
5:00	Office Projects, Meetings and Planning (Blue)
5:30	Daily Wrap Up & Planning for Tomorrow (Blue)
6:00	Travel Time (Yellow)
6:30	Dinner Preparation (Purple)
7:00	Dinner (Purple)
7:30	Self, Partner & Family Activities (Purple)
8:00	Self, Partner & Family Activities (Purple)
8:30	Self, Partner & Family Activities (Purple)
9:00	Self, Partner & Family Activities (Purple)
9:30	Evening Grooming (Pink)
10:00	Bedtime (Pink)

When my clients complete this exercise, it becomes clear that there is an imbalance between what they want in their life and where they are spending their time. They can easily see where the time is going and how it results in an upside-down pyramid. To recreate the balance in your day and invert the pyramid, begin from your Life Priorities and Life Navigational Road Maps. Begin this exercise by blocking out time on your calendar to make sure your well-being becomes and remains a priority in your life. If you find there are areas that are consuming too much time (i.e., housecleaning, laundry, errands, and lawn care, etc.), consider if there are ways to outsource that task to regain the time for the things you love and want more of in your life (i.e., family, friends, hobbies, travel, health, etc.).

What does your "New, Integrated Day" look like with you being first? Fill in your colors!

Today	"My Ideal Day ~ Me First!"
5:00	
5:30	
6:00	
6:30	
7:00	
7:30	
8:00	
8:30	
9:00	
9:30	
10:00	
10:30	
11:00	
11:30	
12:00	
12:30	
1:00	
1:30	
2:00	
2:30	
3:00	
3:30	
4:00	
4:30	
5:00	
5:30	
6:00	
6:30	
7:00	
7:30	
8:00	
8:30	
9:00	
9:30	
10:00	

CREATE A FINANCIAL PLAN

It is amazing how many individuals do not have a financial plan that creates freedom and independence. Too many individuals live month-to-month or worse, paycheck to paycheck. Even the affluent has a tendency to live at or beyond their means. The result—stress, worry, and fear around money, fear about losing their homes or being able to afford healthcare if they lose their jobs; fear about providing for their families' needs. Living your life from this place is not good for your well-being. It is worth discussing how to manage your money from a positive, proactive place and have a financial plan, which is an important part of your holistic integrated Life Navigational Road Map. A financial plan empowers you to achieve everything you want in your life now and in the future. There are many great books and materials available on this topic; however, you should consult with a certified financial planner (CFP) who does not receive commissions for any of the investment suggestions offered. Pay for the consultation to develop an investment strategy that supports your goals. At the end of the consultation, you have no commitment or obligation to this individual and you will have a custom-designed financial plan.

The Vanguard Group shares that "although women may display slightly better investing habits than men, women also tended to have shorter job tenures and lower income than men, on average. So while women were saving and investing a higher percentage of their pay than men, their absolute saving was lower because they typically had a bit less income."[16] Long-term savings are also affected when women take time out of business to raise a family, which is also a factor to consider when designing your financial plan.

I cannot stress enough the importance for you as an individual to have a financial plan and equally as important to have a financial plan with your spouse or partner. Suze Orman speaks to this in great detail in her books, as does David Bach, the author of *Smart Women Finish Rich*. You work hard for your money. You pay taxes, and what you are left with should support your dreams and a lifestyle you want to create.

Most individuals do not know how much income they have coming in and worse how much they have going out. Get comfortable with your financial circumstances and be sure you have a "nest egg," to fall back upon if you lose your job, need to pay for an unexpected household repair or if you incur health-related expenses, etc. Factor the "unexpected" into your financial plan and, if possible, have at least six months of cash available to cover your mortgage and monthly expenses. Factor into your plan fun things in your life like: dinner out with friends, holiday gifts, a fabulous vacation, and other activities that support your lifestyle. It is important to review your financial information on a regular basis to protect yourself from financial harm. It is dynamic and not static. Get your money to work for you. Set financial goals and work to achieve them. It's freeing to have a custom financial plan that creates a safe environment for you but also creates the potential for you to have an abundant life. It's your money. You work hard for it. Don't give it away freely. Be sure it's being spent on things you want to achieve in your life and not just material items that may bring you short-term enjoyment but are not supporting your life dreams.

Here's something to consider: if you purchase a cup of coffee every day for $5.00 and you fall into a 20 percent tax bracket, that means you need to earn $6.00 gross to pay for every cup of coffee. While it nets out to be $1825 per year, you actually need to gross $2190 to cover your daily coffee! That's equal to a vacation or a few car payments or could help pay down your mortgage. If you apply this as an extra mortgage payment, you get the double benefit of reducing the interest you pay to the bank and you pay down your home faster. It's a simple example of how your money can work for you. Be smart about this, ladies, and get your money to work for you!

STAY ACTIVE TO MAINTAIN YOUR HEALTH AND ENERGY

Have you ever watched children play? It's a joyful thing that comes from a place of laughter, fun, and adventure. When did playing turn into "exercise"? Staying healthy is an important part of your well-being, and if you embrace it from the place of "I'm going to go have some fun and play," it takes on a very different perspective than going to the gym to exercise. What if you could incorporate different activities into your life to maintain your health and energy that did not feel like torture? What if you went out to spend time playing tennis, bike riding, swimming, or skating, like a child? Wouldn't that be more fun than running on a treadmill or an elliptical for an hour? How about going for a hike with someone special in your life or a long walk on a beautiful evening? Being healthy and taking care of your well-being can also be accomplished through meditation, yoga, massage, and acupuncture. There are many ways to take great care of you—so go play and have fun!

If this is an area where you have struggled in your life, schedule time with a nutritionist, a personal trainer, or your health-care provider to talk about a program that will work for you in your lifestyle that keeps you healthy, strong, and full of energy. Make this a priority every day. Put yourself first, not last. In doing so you will have more to give to those you love in your life, your career, and other aspects of your life.

REDUCE STRESS

When looking at the root cause of situations women encounter in business, I like to "follow the energy" to assess what's really creating the problem. For many women the stress in their professional lives can be traced back to the limited amount of time available. The lack of time management results in jammed schedules, abrupt conversations, speaking rapidly, and a frantic presence. A few techniques to manage time and in turn reduce the stress and other negative outcomes are:

1. Don't book back-to-back meetings. If this is unavoidable, leave meetings five minutes early to allow you to join the next meeting.
2. Build in 15 minutes to recharge every few hours.
3. Take time to organize things in your life that will make it easy to find what you need without effort. This includes your closet, handbag, bills, laundry, shopping lists, etc.
4. Use technology wherever possible to pay your bills, manage your calendar, or communicate with many people simultaneously.
5. Consider your schedule before committing to anything that will place more demands on your schedule, especially if it is not aligned to your personal or professional goals.
6. Block off time and make it a priority to spend quality time with your spouse, family, or friends.
7. Include time to run errands each week and try to do them in one outing.
8. Find time for you to participate in something spiritual.

Going back to creating our ideal day takes planning. Without planning your day can get away from you and the things you love the most may not get the attention you would like to give. By putting these items into your calendar, it helps you stay organized and keeps the most important things in your life a high priority. It reduces the stress and can gives you back time in your day. Look for ways to organize other areas of your life to reduce stress and give you back valuable time.

Navigating Step 4: Put Yourself First; Not Last

My Journey to the Top — Guide:

- Put Yourself First based on Who You Are, What You Want and Your Life Priorities.

- Change the order of Your Life Pyramid

- Design Your Ideal Work Day which your well-being as a top priority.

- Create a Financial Plan That Supports Your Dreams.

- Keep Active to Maintain Your Health And Energy.

- Reduce Stress. Stay Organized, Outsource What you Can and Don't Overcommit

My Journey to the Top — Notes:

☐ _____

☐ _____

☐ _____

☐ _____

☐ _____

My Journey to the Top — Action Items:

☐ _____

☐ _____

☐ _____

☐ _____

☐ _____

Step 5: Leadership —
Leading From the Front

Effective leaders have a clear sense of direction and values that guide them through their lives, creating a sense of integrity that impacts their decisions, their relationships, and their overall results.

VISIONARY AND STRATEGIC MESSAGE THAT MOTIVATES

To expand upon what we discussed in Steps 1 and 2, the vision of an organization looks out over the horizon in today's business environment between three and five years while the mission of the organization is much closer and can be anywhere from one to thirty-six months. Great leaders always align their message with a long-term vision and mission in mind. Consistently communicating where the organization is heading is important for the directors and managers who are operationalizing the vision and mission to translate it into operational execution. It also ensures that there is "line of sight" connectedness to the individual contributors. Leaders lead from the front.

On your way to the top, this is an important area to master. Not only will your leaders see your ability to align with the broad vision and mission of the company, but they will also know that you possess the ability to motivate others and create alignment that connects them to the broader goals of the organization. It is such an important skill that I recommend you create: (1) your team's vision and mission statement, and (2) your personal vision and mission statement. You want to ensure that both of these align with your leaders from the business context. In doing so, not only are you aligning with your direct management's goals and objectives, but you are also ensuring that you and your team are committed to your leader's success. This goes a long way in your career journey and navigating your way to the top. I recommend that you practice reciting them in the mirror until you can articulate them with ease and confidence. You may also consider posting them within your department and/or adding them to your signature block, which can create a branded tagline for your team in support of the broader company goals and objectives.

LEADERSHIP COMMUNICATIONS

Whether it is a business conversation or in their personal life, observe women as they discuss a topic that is of importance to them. Women will have more energy around the topic and often need to be right (and too often need to point out they are right). Do you think that serves you? While you may be right, did you create allies or enemies? Did it separate you from your colleagues or foster a sense of team? Were you right at the expense of someone else? For female leaders, being *right* can often mean you lose and lose big! If this is an area you recognize in yourself, be aware of when the need to be right arises. Stop talking and assess if it is coming from a place of fear. As you develop your communication style as a leader, it is best not to project it onto others. Once you understand why *needing to be right* is present, you can adjust your messaging back to a place of intellect, interactive conversation and critical thinking.

ENGAGING COMMUNICATION STYLE

Try to view business meetings as a conversation and not a conflict where you are fighting to be heard and acknowledged or to prove that you are right. Women are great conversationalists, and here are a few techniques to share your perspective using a leader's communication style and not commit professional suicide. Try to weave these phrases into your communication style and your ideas will be heard:

I see where John/Sally is going with his/her approach and

- would also like to add this perspective…

- would offer a comparison for consideration…

- would offer a contrasting perspective for discussion…

- suggest we ask, "What if"…

- suggest we ask, "What if we did nothing"…

I would like to acknowledge John/Sally for their approach and

- invite us to also consider…

- would like to further explore…

- believe there is a possibility for…

I agree with John/Sally and

- would like to expand upon it from this angle …

- would also add _____ from my organization's perspective

- would recommend we begin on _____ (date), and you have my commitment of the resources needed to ensure our success

Stop using these words and phrases:

- "I" and use more "we/us/they" (when socializing concepts and enrolling others)
- "Just"
- "It was nothing"
- "I could have done better at …"
- "I'm sorry." Unless you did something wrong; then apologize sincerely and quickly!
- "I feel"
- "I think"

Start using these words/phrases:

- "I recommend" (when making a statement to move forward)
- "What if"
- "What could be possible if"
- "We should explore what the opportunity potential is for …"
- "Let me give that some thought and I'll get back to you tomorrow…"

Leaders are Inclusive and Create Diverse Environments; Everyone Gets to Participate

Leaders over the age of forty look at their careers and business relationships through a different lens than the generation Y and Zers, quoting Claire Shipman of *Good Morning America* and Katty Kay from BBC News, who share that these

> *alphabet-enders have grown up amid significant economic turbulence: the dot com boom and bust, labor force shakeups, corporate greed scandals, the credit card collapse. Coming of age in the era of 9/11 has clearly affected their priorities. They were raised by boomer parents who gave them self-esteem and a desire to have an impact. They're going to be the most high-performing civic minded workforce in the history of the world but they are also going to be the most high maintenance force in the history of the world.* [17]

The younger generation's priorities are very different from those of the baby boomers. Leaders who are not igniting the potential in both of these diverse groups are missing a huge opportunity. Too many leaders surround themselves with like-minded people, suffocating the innovation they could experience in their organization to protect their own comfort levels. This is where many women find themselves today. Women (and individuals from other diversity groups) long for leaders who have evolved beyond the comfortable "like-me" constructs their leaders have created and transformed to see the value diversity brings to an organization. Great leaders embrace diversity and amplify the potential within each of their employees. The opportunity this creates for you is to be the extraordinary leader positioned between the traditional, conservative legacy-leaders, while representing the energy and excitement the younger generation brings to the future. *So what kind of leader do you want to be?* Can you adapt the message and model of the leaders in your organization while still being open and receptive to this young creative force? Can you represent what you want as well as what your employees want when dealing with the legacy leaders? Can you create shifts in the way the traditional leaders think to create new business models for the future? How will you enroll today's leaders to explore transforming themselves, the business, and other leaders to keep the company in the forefront of innovation as well as to attract and retain the best talent in the industry? I submit that if you know who you are and know what you want, you will be able to articulate and enroll other leaders into your vision of what the future can look like by embracing gender and cultural diversity as well as the opportunity for new innovation with today's alphabet generation.

AVOID MICROMANAGEMENT, PERFECTIONISM, AND EMOTIONALISM

If you were to conduct a survey of men and women and directly ask them if they prefer to have a man or a woman manager, you may hear responses like "that's sexist!" From an HR perspective, that may hold some validity. However, when listening to the informal "water cooler talk," you will hear fairly consistently that the majority of the individuals prefer to have male managers, and the reasons are often because women tend to be micromanagers, perfectionists, and bring too much emotion or drama to the office. The evolved businesswoman understands this and eliminates these traits from her business style. Now that you know, let's focus on the course correction to change this immediately!

What individuals are looking for in their leaders is empowerment. Everyone wants to feel included and that their opinions and contributions are valued. When a leader continually dictates step-by-step what must be done and how it must be done, the individuals on their team stop thinking and wait to be told what to do because the leader devalues their opinions. Micromanaging every detail leaves the employee with only the "tasks," and that doesn't feel very rewarding. In addition to it not being motivating, it creates the perception that you are not a leader but a manager. If the latter is associated with your professional brand, it will be difficult to move to higher levels of the organization. A great leader ignites the potential in every employee on their team and empowers them to bring their unique ideas, innovation, and approach to the conversation. What would it look like if everyone on your team were a high performer because as the leader, you ensured every member of the team understood the team's vision and mission as well as the specific initiative that needed to be addressed? What would be different if you allowed them to have ownership on "how" it would be achieved? By empowering them to develop the execution strategy and how to deliver the solution, you, as the leader, can be kept informed based on your timetable (weekly, monthly, quarterly) and your preferred style (e-mail, written report, face-to-face meeting, or a presentation). Just think of the cycles you'll get back and the time you will be able to focus on addressing the more strategic business challenges versus spending your time in the operational details. Keep in touch with your team leaders and meet with them on a regular basis to incorporate your suggestions and provide input. The key to being a leader is to delegate and empower—not to micromanage!

Just as perfectionism can be an impediment to your personal success as well as the speed at which we need to do business, it is equally disempowering to transfer the need to be perfect to your team. As the leader, make a determination on what projects need to get an "A" and what can get a lesser grade. Providing this clarity can minimize the stressors experienced by your team. If all projects require an "A," your team may not be leveraging their energy and focus in the areas that require their attention. Provide them with the guidance needed to set priorities and desired outcomes effectively. Your team will appreciate the clarity and also respect you for giving them back time wherever possible.

Last is the topic of being "emotional." Most women I know really resent this term. For women, when someone says you're being "emotional," what we hear is "don't cry." If we change the term from "being emotional" to "having energy," you can see the issue in a different context. Creating a shift in your perception so that when you feel your energy activated around the topic, one of the questions you, as an evolved businesswoman will ask yourself, is "Why is that getting triggered? Take a deep breath and ask yourself a few questions to understand why a business conversation is activating energy within you. We'll discuss this further in Step 7: Understanding and Managing Conflict.

1. Try to shift the energy to come from a place of intellect by asking questions and not from a place of fear, worry, or emotion.
2. Take a moment to neutralize what you are feeling inside by acknowledging why this is showing up and quiet it within you.
3. What are you afraid will happen? Does this show up at other times? Try to notice a pattern.
4. In addition to asking yourself a few clarifying questions to bring your focus back to the business matters at hand, your energy can be neutralized by asking clarifying questions of the other participants.

UNDERSTAND BUSINESS FINANCE

Many women share that they do not have an affinity toward numbers and this perception is holding them back. While studies have shown that women tend to be more linguistic and men tend to be more mathematically oriented, these are not absolutes and there are many tools available today (i.e., Microsoft Excel) to help you analyze the numbers. There are also great educational programs available to leaders to hone their business finance skills. Many of these courses are available at community colleges, from the American Management Association, or perhaps through your own organization. I strongly encourage all women to invest in themselves, even if it requires you to pay for the course yourself. Take a business finance course or two. It is the language of business, and it is important to understand how to run a profitable organization and bring shareholder value. Without this knowledge, you will be limited as to how far you can navigate to the top. Make this a priority in your career development and consider finding a mentor who has a strong business finance background to develop this very important business-leadership capability.

CREATE MENTEE PROJECT OPPORTUNITIES

A concept that creates a win-win scenario is to enroll mentees and direct reports to lead projects that are of interest to them and their career goals. This model allows you to provide mentorship and coaching while helping them gain exposure to broader business perspectives. What's great about this model is that they get exposure to different aspects of the business environment and the opportunity to present to other leaders. Wise leaders who use this model benefit in a few ways:

1. You get tactical help on a project that is important to you.
2. You are investing in others and their career goals.
3. You will be sought out as someone who cultivates others.
4. You get back cycles to work on other strategic initiatives.
5. You will be viewed as an empowering leader.
6. It helps you scale.

BE A ROLE MODEL FOR OTHERS TO EMULATE

An organization will often emulate the attitude and energy of their leaders. This creates a wonderful opportunity for you to "lead by example" for everyone in your organization. For women joining the workforce and those who aspire to climb the ladder of success, be their role model and share with them the attributes great leaders possess. Help the hone their leadership skills and pay-it-forward by sharing the "tough love" messages in this book and the lessons you learned on your journey as a rising-leader as well as when you reach the board room.

Navigating Step 5: Leadership — Leading from the Front

My Journey to the Top — Guide:

- Visionary and Strategic Messaging that Motivates.

- Support your Leaders and Team's Success

- Develop Excellent Leadership Communications Skills that Engage Others

- Avoid Micromanagement, Perfectionism, and Emotionalism.

- Understand Business Finance. It's the language of business.

- Create Mentee/Employee Project Partnerships.

- Be a Role Model for Others to Emulate.

My Journey to the Top — Notes:

☐ _____

☐ _____

☐ _____

☐ _____

☐ _____

My Journey to the Top — Action Items:

☐ _____

☐ _____

☐ _____

☐ _____

☐ _____

Step 6: Meet People Where They Are

We are all "one of a kind." This presents an excellent opportunity to work with many diverse individuals to develop a broader view of the world, business strategies, and the people around us. You will be a better leader and richer for the experience.

LEADERS FOCUS ON PEOPLE

Aren't people fascinating? Just as no two snowflakes are alike, the uniqueness of our DNA combined with our life experiences create our one-of-a-kind way of being. Every encounter with someone different than us culturally, ethnically, socially, or by gender or age is a gift. Do you recall when you were a child and you went through the "why" phase? Or perhaps you have a young child at home and recall how much fun that phase is! Children are curious and are eager to learn about everything around them. They fearlessly ask questions about everything they do not understand. As a leader, I encourage you to find that part of who you are at every possible opportunity. Seek out individuals who are different from you and spend time to get to know them and really "be" with them. It will make you a better leader and a better, wiser human being who embraces diversity.

GET CURIOUS ABOUT THOSE AROUND YOU.

I had an opportunity to spend three weeks in Kathmandu, Nepal. There was not one aspect of that trip that aligned with what I knew and experienced in my daily life in the United States. The gift I received was nonstop transformation, embracing everything and everyone who were completely different from me. I learned so much from the beautiful, peaceful Nepalese people (who are predominantly Hindu and Buddhists) in what is categorized as a "developing country." Every moment, every experience, and every encounter was an opportunity to be completely open to the experience and what I could learn during my time with them.

In the context of meeting people where they are, there I was—completely at the mercy of the people and the journey I was to experience. The gift I received was profound, and in order to truly embrace the experience, I had to surrender completely to the environment. In doing so my eyes were opened about my own limitations in the way I interacted with people. For example, I entered the country with a good education, wisdom, and construct from being raised in the United States. Applying my learnings and experiences, I immediately could see *all the things that were broken* about Nepal and how some of their challenges could be solved—but guess what, they do not need to be fixed! I was imposing my interpretations, judgments, and perceptions and ways of being onto who they were, which prevented me from being connected with them. Don't get me wrong—the environment and government infrastructure were completely broken. But the people did not need to be fixed, and some of what Americans would deem as broken wasn't broken at all. I needed to transform, and in order for me to do this, I needed to be humble and ask lots of questions about their history, culture, religion, and politics and connect with the people. What I learned from this trip (and from my life's journey) that can be incorporated into business was: Can we just "be" with those around us from a place of non-judgment and appreciate the unique attributes and contributions everyone can make and then ignite all of their potential? I needed to "meet them where they were" to create new possibilities in my life and leadership style.

BE A DIVERSITY AND INCLUSION LEADER

In my coaching practice, I witness many leaders who surround themselves with similar leaders, creating a limited environment with like-minded thinking, little or no conflict, and smooth uninterrupted sailing. After all, there is enough stress in their day — right? Why compound it by adding diversity issues that will challenge them as a leader? That is where they are comfortable as a leader; however it can stifle innovation and creativity. It creates an environment of "more of the same" and does not represent the beautiful tapestry of diverse individuals we have in the workplace. Do you have the courage to have leaders on your team who don't think like you, dress like you, or want to be your "yes" man or woman? Many leaders say yes but cannot pass this diversity assessment. Take a look around you:

1. How diverse is your leadership team?
2. How diverse are the members of your organization?
3. What is the percentage of gender diversity?
4. What is the percentage of ethnic diversity?
5. How many grew up in a different socioeconomic status?
6. How many have a different sexual orientation?
7. For how many is English is their second language?
8. Are you promoting individuals of diversity?
9. Do you mentor individuals of diversity?
10. What is the composition of your friends?

Are you open to transform yourself to embrace inclusion and diversity on your team? Are you creating a culture that fosters diverse thinking and inclusion of everyone? In today's global environment, organizations that embrace different points of view will be the leaders in the future.

EMBRACE DIVERSE BACKGROUNDS AND LIFE EXPERIENCES

My international clients are often frustrated when working with American leaders because they feel that Americans are impatient and often do not allow them to finish their thoughts. This creates a barrier for individuals to provide valuable input into the conversation. I encourage you as a leader to ensure that everyone gets to participate. It is particularly important to surround yourself with diverse thinkers from a variety of cultures and ethnicities, genders, and ages and hear what they have to say. For those who are reserved during meetings in offering their perspective, engage them directly and ask them for their thoughts. This is the role of the leader—to create an environment where everyone's opinion is heard and discussed.

I participated in meetings in Germany as a part of a global team for Siemens Medical developing a new website that focused on creating awareness around integrated health management by incorporating digital images and medical reports into an electronic health record. During my visits to Germany, I was a "diversity" individual but never felt my ideas were not heard; I never felt left behind or excluded. Our team had individuals from around the world representing diversity in age, gender, religion and cultural backgrounds. We took time to ensure we all remained on the same page and worked through our language, culture, and business differences. In doing so, we were united in our commitment to the project's success and, even more so, each other's success. What would be possible if all leaders adopted this model? What if all leaders took ownership of ensuring that the team "meet people where they are" and cultivated an inclusive environment? Engage individual team members and ask questions to learn more about them so you can support them in achieving their goals and understand how they would like to be engaged in the discussion in a way that works for them.

Invite diversity to your teams and cultivate an environment where patience is respected and everyone's voice and ideas are heard. Take the time to appreciate the differences and celebrate the cultural, social, and other unique gifts every individual brings. By embracing diverse backgrounds, the entire team will receive the gift of a broader worldview and an appreciation that being a part of a United States based company doesn't mean we cannot be open to ideas from extraordinary innovators who may be from another country or culture.

CREATE AN ENVIRONMENT FOR EVERYONE'S IDEAS AND PERSPECTIVES TO BE HEARD

Have you ever been in a meeting where one individual dominates the conversation? Don't get me wrong—I love it when a leader or individual has an inspirational or motivational message for the group. But I'm referring to the individual who can be a bit forceful or controlling or needs to be right. Did you ever notice the body language of the individuals who have to sit through that meeting? I invite you to pay close attention during your next meeting, and what you will most likely find when an individual dominates the meeting, is that the remaining individuals disengage or suffer through it. For them, they just want the meeting to end. There's no win for them to take on the issue with the dominant player. For them, it's not worth "dying on that hill" or "fighting that fight," and everyone loses—the quiet sufferers lose, the team loses by not having everyone's input, and the company loses because they're not receiving the maximum benefit, contribution, and passion from their employees. As a result, the customer loses because everyone's ideas are not being heard. If this is occurring in your organization, it presents an opportunity for you to change the dynamics and create a new culture where all voices are heard and no ideas are left behind. Meet with the individual who tends to dominate the meeting and share your vision of cultivating a more collaborative, inclusive environment and ask for their support to create this type of environment during meetings. By enrolling that individual, it may cause them to adapt their style and take on a leadership role to engage others in the meeting and, as a result, will be less dominant.

Navigating Step 6: Meet People Where They Are

My Journey to the Top — Guide:

- Leaders Focus on People. Managers Focus on Process.
- Get Curious About Those Around You.
- Embrace Diverse Backgrounds and Life Experiences — Cultural, Religious, Social, Gender, Age, Ethnicity
- Be a Diversity and Inclusion Leader. Diversity Creates Innovative Results
- Create an Environment for Everyone's Ideas and Perspectives to Be Heard.
- Leaders Are Inclusive—Everyone Gets to Participate.

My Journey to the Top — Notes:

☐ _____

☐ _____

☐ _____

☐ _____

☐ _____

My Journey to the Top — Action Items:

☐ _____

☐ _____

☐ _____

☐ _____

☐ _____

Step 7: Understanding and Managing Conflict

Conflict is an inevitable part of the workplace. Leverage differing opinions, ideas, and expectations to create constructive conversation and controversy to increase creativity.

CONFLICT OR INTERPRETATION?

This is one of the more complicated areas to discuss on a woman's journey to the top. How women define what conflict means and their interpretation of what a conflict is creates their perception and subsequently their response. This interpretation and perception creation activates energy inside women (often labeled as "being emotional"). Women get activated from a place of fear. This is a unique and personal experience for every individual based on our life experience and adaptation or conditioning to survive. It begins a process within us that prepares us for action from a place of fear. This is referred to as "fight, flight, or freeze," which defines changes your body goes through in response to stress. These changes may include an increase in heart rate, a narrowing of vision, muscle tension, sweating, and more sensitive hearing. I share this background as a foundation of what happens to you physiologically when you interpret that the business conversation is a "conflict."

What could be possible if you viewed business conversations as an opportunity to discuss and explore different perspectives, develop new solutions, and embrace input from others? Can you create a shift by identifying that business conversations revolve around data or content (which has no energy or emotion)? If you can look at these interactions from a place of discussions to refine or clarify the data or content, you are empowered to reinterpret what is happening. You can shift your interpretation to understand that this is not a conflict. If you look at it from the perspective that we all bring diverse backgrounds, perspectives, styles, and approaches into a meeting and you appreciate those differences and focus on *what is being said* and *not how it is said*, you can focus on the message and not the energy or emotion attached to the message. Emotion and judgment at this level of the game are an impediment to business success. They create an environment that thwarts an open exchange of ideas because there is emotion present. Focus on the data and not the message delivery. Check your emotions to take them out of the conversation.

When you believe you are in conflict, I want you to ask yourself, *Is this really a conflict—a fight or an argument—or is it my interpretation*? From there you can ask yourself what you win in this business setting if you come from a place of fear (which triggers fight, flight, or freeze)? Your response will most likely be that there is no win or benefit for you. So the natural follow-up question becomes what is the cost you were paying for having this interpretation? [18] If you are activated and you're presenting energy around the issue, most likely you are paying a big cost. It may manifest itself in a variety of ways, but one of them is the perception of others that you are "too emotional," and that label can be the curse of death for you to move to senior positions of management.

When you perceive there is a conflict, take a deep breath, pause, and consider these questions to create the shift from emotion to intellect and refocus on the business outcomes:

1. What is that about? Why am I activated around this topic?
2. Have I activated something in the other individual?
3. Ask questions to explore and discuss to understand their perspective.
4. Is this really a conflict I need to manage, or is it an interpretation from fear?
5. Can I shift my mindset from "conflict" to "this is a business discussion"? If not:
   a. What am I winning by coming from a place of fight, flight, or freeze?
   b. What is the cost I am paying?
6. Ask open and exploratory questions in support of finding a solution.

It Really Is a Conflict

What do we do when there truly is conflict in the workplace? In addition to asking the questions above, it is important to realize that we can only manage our words, our actions, and ourselves. Don't make it about the other person and what they are doing wrong or about your opinion of them. It presents you with an opportunity to ask exploratory business questions and not come from a place of emotion or fear.

Before asking any questions, compose yourself and get into your confident leader position to shift from emotion to intellect (review more details in Step 3 on Executive Presence):

1. Use silence to create an intentional pause. Very powerful!
2. Take a deep breath (from your diaphragm) and, more importantly, exhale deeply. This gives you time to reflect on your response. It also increases the oxygen into your body, which reduces stress.
3. Deliver a solution-focused response. Do not tell a story.
4. Close with a question requesting alignment, support, or consensus. If this is not achieved, ask another question to see what additional information you can provide and then reclose.

Use more "I statements" that focus on what you need. For example:

As we focus on the solution to this issue:

- I recommend _____.

- I need _____ resources and can have this addressed by _____.

- I propose we implement _____ and begin right away. I'll take responsibility for leading the effort.

How you respond during times of conflict and tension is a true indicator of your business leadership abilities. Conflict provides you with an opportunity to reconnect and enroll others to support the project, initiative or goal outcomes. With every promotion, the potential for stress increases as the business challenges will become more strategic and have a broader impact across the organization; you also must factor in how your strategy is going to increase shareholder value. In order to adapt to this intellectual way of being, go toward the issue—do not avoid it. Ask great questions, offer solutions, and ask for the enrollment of your colleagues.

GET OVER IT

One of the most important pieces of advice I can offer to women is to get over any business conflicts fast and not hold any grudges. It is a business conversation. How is it that men can have a healthy debate or disagreement and then grab a beer after work? Ask anyone their opinion on how women handle disagreements and the claw-scratching visual and sound effects of a catfight are demonstrated. Women need to evolve beyond this and change the perception of how women handle business conflict in general. In addition, women need to pay particular attention to how conflict between women affects them. Too many women dig in and hold grudges against other women as if it is a fight to the death. The dynamics are fascinating. In one context, women are nurturing, loving and cultivate wonderful friendships; however in business, woman-to-woman relationships often show up as a competition. I have read a variety of theories based on studies that have been conducted and regardless of why this behavior exists, it is within a woman's control to change it! Now that you know women have this tendency and it is observed in the workplace in a negative way, you are empowered to create the change within yourself to stop it!

Equally as important is to eliminate gossip and negativity toward other women. Women tend to hold other women back and not offer them a hand to lift them up. Not only does it hurt the accused or victim of the gossip, but the accuser is looked upon negatively also! This is an behavior women must stop immediately!

Unfortunately, women are often observed gossiping or creating drama that creates conflict in the workplace. Practice adopting this philosophy: *if you are not willing to take an individual aside and have a conversation with them directly to resolve your issue, don't have the conversation with anyone else about it or them.*

NAVIGATING STEP 7: UNDERSTANDING AND MANAGING CONFLICT

MY JOURNEY TO THE TOP — GUIDE:

- Is it really a Conflict or your Interpretation?
- When Conflict Arises, Ask Yourself:
    - What's That About?"
    - What Is Being Triggered in You or in Others?
    - Ask Questions to Explore and Discuss. `
    - Present Solutions.
    - Bring Your Intellect and Not Emotion to the Discussion.
- Manage Yourself, Your Words, and Your Actions.
- Get Over It Fast. Don't Hold Grudges. Come Fresh to Each Meeting and Each Individual Encounter.
- Support Women during Conflict and Eliminate Gossip.

MY JOURNEY TO THE TOP — NOTES:

- ☐ _____
- ☐ _____
- ☐ _____
- ☐ _____
- ☐ _____

MY JOURNEY TO THE TOP — ACTION ITEMS:

- ☐ _____
- ☐ _____
- ☐ _____
- ☐ _____
- ☐ _____

Step 8: 360° Leaders Give Back

In addition to your own journey of development, giving back to others, those of diversity and women, cultivates future women leaders, broadens your ability to be a great leader, and expands your network.

In addition to leading from the front, executives understand the importance of being a 360° leader by giving back through mentorships, community outreach, board membership and thought leadership within their industry.

CORPORATE EMPLOYEES

There are many ways you can give back. In the corporate environment this often will manifest itself in being a mentor or coach. Many organizations have employee resource groups (ERGs) or similar organizations that align with their diversity and inclusion goals. For example, an ERG is not limited to who can participate, but its focus will align with the goals of the group: women, African-American, Latinos, Gay, Lesbian, and Transgender, etc. It's an excellent way as a leader to align with the outcomes the group is trying to achieved by presenting to them or understanding the issues they care about. Get involved with employee resource groups and let them know you are a leader who hears them, supports them, and will help them achieve their goals.

CORPORATE-ALIGNED CHARITABLE ORGANIZATIONS

You can also align with corporate philanthropic initiatives like the United Way or the Red Cross or Habitat for Humanity, which focus on the corporate identity in alignment with larger nationally identified nonprofits. Each organization is different, so check the websites concerning corporate social responsibility, giving back, philanthropy, or community outreach to see which corporate initiatives align with your giving spirit.

Join a Nonprofit Board

Joining the board of a nonprofit, philanthropic organization is a wonderful way for you to couple your business experience with your corporate brand where you can really make a difference. On the corporate side, aren't they fortunate to have woman leader taking their brand into the community! This creates a tremendous opportunity for you to align your company's mission with the values of the philanthropic community and something you are passionate about. This trifecta provides a multitude of benefits for the company, the philanthropic organization, you and most importantly also for the individuals who benefit from your participation.

Organize Events in Your Region or Department.

While I was at Cisco, I organized many philanthropic events, primarily with the extraordinary support of the employees. Of the many I had the privilege of organizing, the event that represents this type of integrated outreach best was a partnership developed between the Department of Veteran Affairs, Cisco, and their federal government partners, The Verizon Center and Washington Mystics (a women's professional basketball team). The mission of this event was to make a difference in the lives of our active military members who were transitioning back to civilian life and veterans to find them jobs.

I was honored to work with leaders in the Department of Veterans Affairs Transition Office in 2010 and was also involved in the many veteran outreach efforts the Cisco Veterans employees organized throughout the year to support our troops. While I am not a veteran, I have family members and friends who are. What they experienced and witnessed many of us will never be able to truly comprehend. This event was born out of seeing veterans every day at the VA hospitals and understanding that these are the most dedicated, loyal, hard-working, intensely trained individuals you will ever meet, and they were struggling to navigate the waters to find work as a civilian. Surely we could fix that! All it would take is to send out a rallying cry to retired Lt. General Steven Boutelle, Vice President at Cisco, and the Cisco Veterans, who work tirelessly to develop mentorship and career-transitioning programs. If you ever want to get something done, engage members of our military and veteran community! The Cisco Veterans and members of Cisco Federal enthusiastically jumped in to this outreach program to support our men and women who serve. For several months, the team of Cisco Veterans and others who support our veterans came together to develop a career fair that provided our veterans with free tickets to enjoy a Washington Mystics basketball game on Military Appreciation Day while visiting the largest corporations in the Washington, DC area to talk about career transitioning and open positions in their organization. Every day the Cisco Veterans are doing something extraordinary for those who serve and for our veterans. And I was honored to lead the team to create this integrated Military Appreciation and Career Fair event, which has become an annual event at the Verizon Center. A few months after the event, Cisco and several other major corporations came together to form the 100,000 Mission to create jobs for our veterans. It's great to know that our event played a small role in support of larger initiatives in service to our veterans!

The increase in civic-minded individuals joining corporations today presents a tremendous opportunity for women who are naturally involved in philanthropic events with their children, with the community, or personally to have a level of impact as leaders and to represent the corporation in making a difference in the lives of so many and also serving as role models to our youth who see the value in giving back.

Find a cause and get behind it. If you're able to align your company's goals with something you love and have a positive impact in the community everybody wins. If you're interested in paying it forward and supporting the next generation of women leaders who will follow behind you, you may consider finding nonprofit organizations whose mission is to cultivate young girls to become "strong, smart, and bold," like Girls, Inc., which provides research-based education to all girls and many who are diverse and socioeconomically impacted.

Industry-Specific Organizations

Another extraordinary way to give back while receiving significant professional benefit is to join the leadership team of a community-based organization that aligns with your professional goals. For example, if you are a woman leader in the area of technology, you may consider joining a professional-development organization whose mission is to develop women leaders in technology. Of course any organization would benefit tremendously by having an extraordinary female executive like you as a member of their leadership team to provide relevant content to their members. It is an excellent résumé builder, a way to have your brand recognized as a credible source and put you in a position of being a sought-after subject matter expert in the field. While networking is very good, being a leader and speaker within your industry catapults your visibility to the highest level and will place you in demand for networking and sponsorship opportunities.

EXECUTIVE SPONSORSHIP & PARTICIPATION

It is important for women to balance the amount of philanthropy work they are doing and the perception it creates in business, especially around strong leaders who may be focused primarily on revenue generation and may perceive other activities as a distraction. Some leaders, especially during tough economic times, may view anyone who has time for non-revenue-generating activities as disconnected from the mission. Ensure that you have socialized your approach with your leaders, get their sponsorship, and whenever possible, include them. Having them on your team, creating a few photo opportunities for them, or helping the organization look great will be of value to them. Know the rules and be sure your leaders support you before investing your time.

Most corporations do not have specific groups for men within their employee resource groups as they do for gender, ethic, and other groups that tend to support minority and diversity groups. To address this, organizations have shifted from using the term "diversity" to "inclusion" to ensure that men do not feel excluded. Unfortunately, it does not really meet what men may have been looking for, and as a result men still feel excluded. When everyone is invited to participate regardless of the group's focus, it results in a more interesting group. If men are being excluded from the groups you are involved in, reach out and include them in your activities, events, and initiatives. Ask them if they would like to get to get involved in areas that are important to them. Great leaders ensure everyone is included and has the opportunity to participate.

Navigating Step 8: 360° Leaders Give Back

My Journey to the Top — Guide:

- Participate in Philanthropic Opportunities and join Boards that Combine your Passion with your Company's Goals to have an Impact in the Community.

- Develop the Next Generation of Leaders. Get Involved with Girls and Women Organizations. Develop Strong Women Leaders.

- Join Industry Organizations as a Thought Leader.

- Seek Executive Sponsorship for your Philanthropic, Thought Leadership and Mentorship engagements.

- Be an Inclusive leader and reach out to men to participate in diversity groups.

My Journey to the Top — Notes:

☐ _____

☐ _____

☐ _____

☐ _____

☐ _____

My Journey to the Top — Action Items:

☐ _____

☐ _____

☐ _____

☐ _____

☐ _____

Step 9: Develop Relationships with a Purpose

Women possess the innate gifts to develop strong friendships, nurture family members, and care for others and should extend these gifts to achieve their professional and personal goals.

You'll notice that I did not refer to this step as networking. This is done with intent and forethought. While the industry refers to networking as individuals getting together with to make connections and promote business, I'd like to create a shift here for women—that it's all about developing relationships with a purpose. This may be achieved through networking; however, it is how you build those relationships that are important. This is an area where men and women differ greatly. When women network, the way we build trust and long-term, sustained relationships is by first getting to know each other. It may be small talk around family events, fashion trends, or current events. We like to get to know people at a more human-interest level before jumping right into the business conversation. This is how women prefer to identify how we are relevant to one another and how we can develop a business relationship. We establish trust in this process and determine similar interests as well as compare and contrast our personality types. Women are conversationalists, and we enjoy the journey of connecting by getting to know each other *before* we delve into business.

While this may be women's preferred method of networking and a natural way of being for us, in business it can be misunderstood and perceived as weakness. A word of caution—some male leaders look upon this as ineffective and not impactful to business. The parallel experience for them may be to talk about sporting events or the stock market, which is a natural part of how men relate to one another. While both men and women enjoy connecting through non-business-related conversation, it is what we are discussing and how it is perceived in terms of relevancy to future business relationships that differs. Most importantly, it is the transition from casual conversation to getting down to business.

The perception men have is that women struggle to move the conversation beyond the introductory phase of networking to identify where the business opportunity exists and ask for the follow-up meeting, create alignment for a joint business venture, or get an investment. This is the key differentiator about the way that men and women network and build their business relationships. Men move quickly through the introductory conversation to understand how they relate to one another to find the synergy in business. The goal is to find where they can be impactful to each other's business outcomes and move forward to look for opportunities that are mutually beneficial.

1. When you network take it to the next level to find mutual business relevancy.
2. Can you get to know someone and move toward understanding how you can be impactful to each other's business?
3. Why are you relevant to them?
4. Why should any business leader partner with you?
5. Do you take time to follow up after the conversation?

It is important to understand that networking is not meant only for the social aspect but to move to the next phase of revenue generation or other business impact area. How women network and the results we achieve brands us. The type of events we attend in support of networking brands us. I encourage you to give some thought from a business perspective to where you are networking and ensure that it aligns with where you want your brand represented. What are the most impactful organizations for you to network that bring real impact to your business, your leaders, and your aspirational goals to make it to the top? With the limited amount of time you have, choose wisely and network effectively.

PLACES TO DEVELOP RELATIONSHIPS WITH A PURPOSE

WITHIN YOUR ORGANIZATION

It is important to your success to build relationships with a purpose within your organization. They can take on many forms, with the two most common being the following:

1. Informal. This can consist of a feedback session from specific interaction or be based on an individual's area of expertise.
2. Formal. This can take the form of regularly scheduled meetings with an agreement, plan, or objective defined. Some formal mentorships create a contract that both individuals sign outlining their commitment to each other and their success.

Every encounter presents you with an opportunity to engage with leaders in your organization and to continually ask for additional follow-up interactions to cultivate your relationship and gain visibility. In addition to their mentorship, it's an opportunity for them to get to know you and for you to communicate on an ongoing basis your value to the organization as a major player in their future. Seize every opportunity to engage with your senior executives, and always schedule a follow-up meeting to stay relevant to them. Come prepared with topics that are relevant to them, share your ideas on how you can be impactful to the business, ask for their feedback, and always let them know you will touch base with them again in a few months. Send a thank-you note after the meeting capturing the salient points.

WITHIN INDUSTRY

Being present at the right industry events is time extremely well spent. This will vary from industry to industry, so you'll need to do a little research on which organizations are having the most impact to innovation, solutions, partnerships, and business outcomes. Ask others in your industry what they would recommend. If you only have time to join one industry organization in support of building the right relationships, which one would it be and why? This will vary depending upon your goals and your career plans. Selecting an industry organization that ties back into increased visibility for your brand across the industry, as well as within your company, can be the best investment you can make with your free time. Your time is valuable, your brand is important, and it's up to you to use your time wisely to build the right relationships in support of your long-term life and career goals. A lack of focus can take you off course. Take time to select the right industry organizations to meet your goals.

WITH YOUR CLIENTS AND CUSTOMERS

Develop a trusted-advisor relationship with your clients and customers by aligning with their top business initiatives, goals and challenges. Understand the problems they are trying to solve, why it is important for them to solve them and what happens if they are not solved. Explore with them what success looks like and how they are personally measured when the goal is achieved. Bring value by offering ideas, resources and relationships in support of their success. Be a part of providing ideas in support of the solution. In doing so, you will develop a partnership with your clients based on trust — a relationship with a purpose that has impact.

LEVERAGE YOUR NETWORK

A masterful relationship builder leverages their network dynamically by connecting with individuals based on the topic and by connecting others who are relevant to each other. As you move up the ladder of success and into the executive ranks, leaders need to develop the delicate balance of managing who moves in and out of your spheres of influence. You will be sought out with requests for your time, guidance, and recommendations. It's a wonderful problem to have as a power relationship builder and executive. When you get to this level, you need to protect your time, and it's important to learn the art of saying "no" gracefully. As an executive, you need to ensure that your priorities are clear and the relationships that are most impactful to your goals receive the highest priority. Women who struggle with saying "no" find themselves spread too thin, unable to be effective at what is important to them, and overstressed. No one wins in this scenario. Leaders are able to communicate from a place of humility and grace with a warm smile, that while their current commitments require their focus, they would explore the opportunity again at some point in the future. It is a great structure to say "no" with support for what could be possible in the future.

REQUESTS FOR ACCESS TO YOUR NETWORK

What do you do when there isn't alignment between you and another individual that would like to develop a relationship? It is important to let those who seek access to you or individuals in your network that you appreciate them, will keep their information in your systems, and will reach out to them when the opportunity arises. This model keeps the door open and provides an opportunity for ongoing dialogue when the time is right. Closing the door with a firm no or completely ignoring the request will not serve you well on your long-term leadership and executive journey. It may work negatively against your brand, and we all know that in this small world, paths have the potential to cross again. The opportunity for you is to leave a great impression, and you may have a chance to do business together in the future.

ONLINE

There are many ways to build business relationships online through social networking, with the most prominently known being "LinkedIn." With the ability to connect to an unlimited number of individuals, the question becomes what is your value proposition. Who do you need to connect with and why? LinkedIn has become our contact-management system, replacing the Rolodex and electronic contact systems. Almost every business relationship I have is a connection on LinkedIn. It is also an excellent source to obtain a historical perspective on individuals from their accomplishments, biography, and areas of interest. The real power of LinkedIn comes from participating in discussions within groups, sharing relevant content with those groups, and also sending personal communications to individuals in your network.

When you look at being relevant to your LinkedIn network, the interconnection between other social-networking sites creates an opportunity for you to provide one update that broadcasts to many mediums. By way of example, if you have a blog you can post an update to your blog that acts as a central repository that is indexed by the search engines (i.e., Google, Yahoo, and Bing) and can then be shared with several social networking sites like Twitter, Facebook, and LinkedIn, the most prominent social networking sites. This is the model I recommend if you would like to become a subject matter expert on a topic. You would own the blog and have several vehicles to communicate the updates to your network. What's great about this model is that you can tie it back to the other methods of building relationships with a purpose. From a business perspective if you blog about topics that are relevant to your company, you bring value to them. That value would then transcend into the industry with you being a thought leader on that topic, which in turn results in your becoming viewed as a subject matter expert who is sought after across the industry.

INFLUENTIAL/THOUGHT LEADERS

Is your network balanced? Do you have strong relationships with your peers? How about those with more senior titles? Are you spending time with individuals who are like you, or are you stretching yourself and engaging with leaders in other industries or diversities? Far too often we stay in our comfort zone with individuals who are similar to ourselves. This model is not serving you and your aspirational goals. Do you have the courage to reach out to others and establish relationships where you could bring value to them? You never know—your relationship may turn out to be your next customer, employer, or business partnership.

GREAT WOMEN LEADERS

In addition to your broad networking strategy, explore those who you believe are the great women leaders in your industry, community, and generation. You have nothing to lose by reaching out to these strong women of influence, intellect, and power by introducing yourself from a place of relevancy and ask if they will mentor you. The worst thing that could happen is they say no, and that won't kill you! You may miss the opportunity of a lifetime by not asking. Seek them out and tell them how much you appreciate who they are and what they're accomplishing. Share with them what you are achieving in your life and how it is relevant to them. Ask for their support, and be specific about what you need. You never know what the answer will be unless you do so.

A great way to interact with women leaders is to attend workshops specifically designed for women. Not only will they leave you inspired and motivated, but you will have an opportunity to introduce yourself directly to explore if there is synergy with your goals. These workshops often include breakout sessions on topics that are important to women as well as many authors who attend to promote their books. Spending time with confident women leaders creates an environment for you to see new possibilities in your life. Being in the presence of confident, motivational women inspired me to find the courage to start my own company and become an author.

In today's connected world, take time to acknowledge other women's accomplishments and support their success. It may be as simple as sharing their work via social networking, purchasing a book or video (and a few for your friends), or amplifying their message in a meeting. Women supporting and promoting women is an excellent way for us to build relationships with purpose that we can leverage to achieve our mutual goals.

LEVERAGING YOUR RELATIONSHIPS FOR MUTUAL BENEFIT

Now that you have an extraordinary portfolio of relationships, individuals who know who you are, why you are relevant to them, and the strong leader you are, now what?

How do we leverage our relationships to ask for what we need? It is amazing how uncomfortable women are when it comes to asking for what they want. It makes them nervous, but why? If the individuals in your network are people you are relevant to and there is value to your relationship, then what you want or need may be something they would want to support. These are your people. You are aligned and connected to some common initiative. The question becomes how you ask.

In addition to asking directly for what you need and how they can support you, another model is to socialize the concept to gain sponsorship for your ideas. Far too often women will work hard, prepare great materials, and deliver compelling presentation but will not socialize their ideas with others in advance to enroll them into their success. This leaves them out there with a great idea and probably an excellent presentation, but without sponsors. Socialize your ideas with others *before* you present them. Ask others what they think about the concept and request their input. This way they feel as if they are included and you will have advocates standing with you. Coming from this place you can then ask for their sponsorship and support with others.

NAVIGATING STEP 9: DEVELOP RELATIONSHIPS WITH A PURPOSE

MY JOURNEY TO THE TOP — GUIDE:

- Develop Relationships with a Purpose.

- Make Time to Meet with Your Leaders, Your Mentors, Your Peers, Influential/Thought Leaders and Great Women Leaders.

- Leverage Your Network For Mutual Benefit.

- Become a Thought Leader. Leverage the Power of Social Networking.

- Socialize Your Ideas, Ask For Feedback and Sponsorship

MY JOURNEY TO THE TOP — NOTES:

- ☐ _____
- ☐ _____
- ☐ _____
- ☐ _____
- ☐ _____

MY JOURNEY TO THE TOP — ACTION ITEMS:

- ☐ _____
- ☐ _____
- ☐ _____
- ☐ _____
- ☐ _____

Step 10: Navigating Your Journey to the Top

Influential leaders understand how to navigate the complex business ecosystem and bring value at all levels of the organization and are sought out for their knowledge.

In this final step we will look at your leadership attributes in a 360° view. First we will explore the art of navigating your career plan through the complex business maze, and second we will look at how to lead teams as the corporate environment changes. In many ways, Step 10 is the culmination and orchestration of all the prior steps. It's about having the clarity and awareness of your surroundings, the players, and the culture to strategically navigate any detours as well as find the express lane to achieve your goals. Your journey may take many years and many different routes. All of the preceding steps come together as one comprehensive, detailed map for both your career and your personal life. When you zoom out to see how all the elements of your life fit together and then align your career goals, you create a beacon to guide you to Your True North—and you have the confidence, clarity, and wisdom to guide the way.

NAVIGATING THE BUSINESS ECOSYSTEM

Throughout your journey the focus has been on who you are, what you want, and how to get there. It is always great when your career plan and goals align with those of your leaders; however, how do you course-correct when it does not? It is important to recognize when the light is (1) green — to accelerate, (2) yellow — to proceed with caution, or (3) red — to change route or come to a complete stop. Understanding where you are requires a great deal of political awareness within your organization, and more so, self-awareness. As you meet with individuals and socialize your career goals, you will gain clarity around the landscape in your organization.

With this clarity comes the opportunity to adapt your message and style based upon the audience and assess where you fit, if your aspirational goals align, and if you need to course-correct. This is where the power of Step 1 comes in. You may receive career advice from wonderful leaders, but in the end it's up to you to decide where your journey is going to take you. Reaching out to other leaders, socializing your career goals, and garnering their input is a part of gathering the data to make an informed decision. Be sure it aligns with what you want and who you are. Let's begin by exploring what your journey looks like when your plan and philosophy are in alignment with those of your leadership.

CREATE VELOCITY AND ACCELERATE YOUR PLAN

Aligning with your leaders creates an environment for high performance and velocity to make an impact. Leveraging this positive environment allows you to socialize your career plans and ideas with others who are in alignment with your goals.

1. Meet with individuals in the organization and share with them your aspirational career goals. Ask them for their guidance and recommendations.
2. Ask how you can learn about the future positions on your career plan.
3. Inquire if there anyone else you should connect with.
4. Train your successor. Too many women are very good at what they do and actually handcuff themselves to their current position, which prevents them from getting promoted. If you are socializing the position you want and training someone to be your successor, you are creating an environment as a leader to make your promotion happen.
5. Volunteer for projects that are aligned with the position you seek.
6. Ask someone to mentor you for that position.
7. Meet with the individual who is currently in the position, if possible, and see how you can support their career plan, which in turn may result in your success.

When your work environment provides you with the opportunity to create velocity for your career plan, leverage the synergies that exist culturally and politically for you and your team—amplifying their success, creating visibility for them, and taking time to celebrate their accomplishments. In this positively aligned environment, put the pedal to the metal and accelerate your plan!

DIFFERING PATHS

How do you proceed when you are not aligned with your leaders or their vision? It is important to understand office politics, which will be different for every organization. Imagine you are a Republican in a room full of Democrats (or vice versa) and you are trying to gain support for an idea or gain sponsorship for a position. It will be more challenging to achieve than if you were in a room of similar party members. Be sure to align your message with your audience and understand the players and their agendas and how you can get to a win-win scenario. This requires you to be self-aware and to pay attention to where you fit in the organization and to your relationships and their leadership style. Do not be naïve and think that because you have clarity around "who you are," "what you want," and "how to get there," individuals in this environment will be supportive. Do you have the courage and confidence to recognize when your goals do not align with your leaders? You always have the option of changing your goals, but does that serve you? My clients who are unable to or refuse to see the signs work harder and try to impress their leaders. They are hopeful that one day the project they are working on will get accolades or their leadership team will bring them into the sacred lair. These individuals are resisting or choose to ignore reading the signals, which are perfectly clear, and the longer they resist, the more stressful and toxic the environment becomes. They need to find the courage to move on!

BUILD FLEXIBILITY INTO YOUR PLAN

The intent here is for you to build flexibility into your plan that allows for adaptation based on your journey. If making a course correction will serve you well, then by all means adjust your plan and take the position. You have a choice, and the choice should come from a position of power and clarity based on what you want and who you are. If you are getting advice to take a position you really do not believe aligns with who you are and what you want, graciously decline the offer. Don't settle. Don't take a position because you were afraid or because your boss recommends it. It does not serve you. If you must take a position due to reorganization or restructuring, absolutely do so, and when things settle down, go back to your Life Navigation Road Maps and reassess. If you need to course-correct, do so. Continue to seek out positions that leverage your innate gifts and get you excited to come to work every day. There is no scarcity of jobs regardless of what you hear on the news! Confident individuals who know who they are and what they want always find a place to land. Do not suffer in a position where you are not happy. Find the position you love and ask others in your network to help. Individuals I work with have struggled throughout their professional lives because they try to fit in a role that does not leverage their innate talents. They apply their intellect and wisdom to the position, and they rise to the occasion. But in the end, they still aren't happy.

Let me be clear—I *am* challenging you to strive to get to the next level and get out of your comfort zone; however, if you realize that you are in a position that you are not excited about, reevaluate and modify your plan. Wake up every day and do what you love. You cannot be your best and greatest while you are suffering in a position that does not inspire you. It all goes back to Step 1 and the continual analysis of what is changing in business and how that fits your life goals and your career plan.

LACK OF A PLAN

Unfortunately, too many of my clients retain me after their career takes a wrong turn and they find themselves in a position they do not like, with a leadership team they don't align with or they are unemployed. As we deconstruct how their journey landed them where they are (and begin to create the life they want), what is often revealed is the lack of a solid foundation, so the career advice they received and decisions they made were often based on external influence and not on who they authentically are and what gets them excited in their life. As a result, even the smartest and most successful individuals find themselves in positions that are not the best fit for them and that may put them in harm's way. Paraphrasing what Colin Powell said in Step 1—gather the data, but in the end, go with your gut. If your instincts are telling you that the position is not the right fit, do not let fear and/or the lack of a career plan land you in the wrong position. I encourage you to explore the advice you are receiving and map it to your career plan to see if there is any flexibility between what you designed and what is being proposed. Assess if there truly is a fit and if that position ultimately supports your longer-term goals.

UNDERSTANDING THE PLAYERS

In addition to your career plan, it is important to be savvy about who the players are in your organization: who are the movers and shakers, who are the ones that get things done, who are the trusted advisors, who are the comedians, who are the chosen ones and who are the blockers. Understanding the lay of the land empowers you to participate and align accordingly.

Before going to an important meeting, make a few phone calls and inquire about the individual you are going to meet in an effort to understand:

1. Their background (school they attended, military service, favorite sports team/player, where they grew up and other personal insights, etc.)
2. What they care about in a work context, but also outside of the office (philanthropy, travel, etc.)
3. How they measure success
4. Their top three to five priorities
5. Some of the things that set them off
6. What attributes they look for in their leaders
7. Their leadership style (democratic, command and control, dictatorship, etc.)

LEADING THE WAY—THE RULES KEEP CHANGING

A major part of navigating the complex corporate maze is to understand the current rules as well as stay close to trends that will create the next tipping points and opportunity to lead. It is interesting to note that in 2008 there were only twelve female CEOs in the Fortune 500 companies (2 percent) and in 2012 there are now twenty-one (4 percent).[19] While there is still a ways to go, women are stepping into senior positions that will create new business cultures in the future, and I hope this makes many of the suggestions in this book obsolete! Since 1988, more females have been enrolled in college than men, with a 33 percent difference since 2007.[20] Given the increase of women in the workplace and families needing two incomes, what employees will need in the future may change and leaders will need to adapt. Consider these statistics from the *New York Times* bestseller, *Womenomics:*

- 70 percent of couples in this country are dual income earners

- 63 percent of us believe we don't have enough time for our spouses or partners

- 74 percent of us say we don't have enough time for our children.

- 35 percent of adults are putting significant time toward caring for an elderly relative.

Their findings revealed:

- Half of us want to work fewer hours.

- Half of us would change our schedules.

- More than half would trade money for a day off.

- Three quarters of us want flexible work options.[21]

I called these statistics out because employees are changing the rules. Are you prepared to incorporate new ways of thinking and leading change within your organization? Understanding how to attract talent to your company and more importantly to retain them is essential, especially to women. According to Catalyst, the leading nonprofit membership organization expanding opportunities for women and business,

"Women cite four major reasons for leaving the private sector:

- lack of flexibility (51 percent)
- glass ceiling issues (29 percent)
- unhappiness with the work environment (28 percent), and
- feeling unchallenged in their jobs (22 percent)"[22]

Women-owned businesses are on the rise. As of 2011 there are over 8.3 million women-owned businesses, generating approximately $1.3 trillion in revenues and employing nearly 7 .7 million people. Between 1997 and

2011, when the number of businesses in the United States increased by 34 percent, the number of women-owned firms increased by 50 percent—a rate 1 ½ times the national average."[23]

What these statistics tell me is that women are fearless and are smart and capable leaders, but their needs are not being met in the corporate environment today, and so they leave and hang out their own shingle. This presents an opportunity for women executives to develop new, flexible programs to retain women by supporting their goals to live an integrated, abundant life. Step into your role as a leader and begin a conversation around transformation, offer innovative solutions and help create change your organization will need in the future. Step into your leadership shoes and lead the way.

Navigating Step 10: Navigating Your Journey to the Top

My Journey to the Top — Guide:

- Understand the Business Ecosystem. The Players, Influencers and Blockers.

- Create Velocity for You and Your Team with Aligned Leaders.

- Always Have a Plan and Be Flexible.

- Develop Talent around You So You Can Move to the Next Level.

- Don't Take Positions that Don't Serve you or your Goals.

- Lead Change in Your Organization for the Future.

My Journey to the Top — Notes:

- ☐ _____
- ☐ _____
- ☐ _____
- ☐ _____
- ☐ _____

My Journey to the Top — Action Plan:

- ☐ _____
- ☐ _____
- ☐ _____
- ☐ _____
- ☐ _____

10 Step Survival Guide

A one-page survival guide of the 10 Steps for Success can be downloaded from my website to include in your day planner. www.TrueNorthEnterprise.com

About the Author

Diane Cashin
President and CEO
True North Enterprise

Diane Cashin is a business strategist and executive transformation coach. She is the founder of True North Enterprise, which partners with business executives and individuals to create unprecedented results with speed and velocity.

Throughout her career, Diane has been an influential leader and worked with some of corporate America's biggest names, including overseeing global strategies for Cisco and their collaboration with organizations like: Lockheed Martin, BAE Systems, EMC, The Department of Veteran Affairs and many others.

Diane believes that true leaders are continually learning and never stop evolving, which is why she left success in corporate America to follow her passion and purpose. Her mission is to empower women and transform executives who have what it takes, knows there is more and is trying to get there faster. Diane's gift is shifting others from frustration into a world of possibilities. Her approach comes from an honest, non-judgmental point of view, to help each person achieve his or her full potential.

As a life learner, Diane has an insatiable desire to continually reflect and evaluate the attributes and experiences she needs to improve all aspects of her life. Though Diane was abundantly loved, she grew up sequestered in the poor, inner city neighborhoods of Philadelphia. Living in poverty created an environment of isolation, resulting in a limited view of the world and what was possible. Diane cannot explain what it was about her environment that instilled in her the need to survive, the insatiable desire to always keep learning, and the belief that if you strive to do the right things, good things will happen to you.

It wasn't until Diane was 18 that she had an opportunity to leave her neighborhood, when, the day after high school graduation, she began working as a legal secretary in downtown Philadelphia – "the big city." Interacting with educated, wealthy lawyers she realized she had more to learn and life had so much more to offer. Over the years Diane had had many extraordinary leaders invest their time as a mentor and instill in her that she was smart, capable and that everything is possible. With this foundation, Diane became fearless. She tried many new things, believing in herself and approaching life from the perspective of "what if she couldn't fail" and jumped in. Looking back over 30 years, Diane went from a girl who didn't know what she didn't know, to a world traveler, business executive, and transformation coach. It required breaking out of old habits and limiting beliefs, keeping an open mind, being flexible, and the burning desire to evolve. Though her path to success was often unknown, her line of sight into the future she wanted to create became crystal clear. Most importantly, she was willing to do the work necessary and apply her skills to make those goals a reality.

Diane continually invested in herself obtaining certifications in technology, completing her college degree while working full-time and being a mother, participated in industry and women's organizations, and always sought out leaders as her mentors in support of her career goals.

She created big dreams for her career, which traversed information technology, marketing, sales, and business development across commercial, state, local, federal and global business environments. She thrives on solving complex business problems and quickly rose in the ranks of her career. She was able to use her critical thinking and problem solving skills to partner with business leaders to solve their greatest challenges, and achieve rapid results.

Throughout her accomplishments, she held firm in the belief that she could always improve and pushed the boundaries to expand her capabilities. A core principle Diane followed was being open to hear suggestions and learn lessons that would make her a better, more evolved leader. Her growth was realized with every mistake, providing an opportunity to reflect, analyze, and embrace all the lessons that could be learned.

Through Diane's thirst for knowledge, she made a commitment to receive well-rounded learning experiences from mentorships, formal education, and hard knocks business experience. She received her bachelors of business management degree from the University of Phoenix, and is also a graduate of the Women Unlimited Leadership Program in New York City. These experiences have afforded Diane the opportunity to see business at every level of an organization, providing a sincere appreciation for every person's role in an organizations success. Diane believes that the synergy between all team players is how to win, and great leaders know how to make this happen.

Diane was inspired to write this book after receiving shocking news, which caused her to re-evaluate her purpose and direction in life. After a routine annual physical, pre-cancerous cells were detected and she underwent surgery to remove them. Faced with the harsh reality of what could have been, the goals of what she wanted to accomplish for the rest of her life changed.

This incident provided Diane with yet another opportunity to reflect; however this time reflection came from a very different place. It didn't come from her mind and career plan as a priority; it came from her being, heart and spirit. She reflected on what she needed to learn from this experience and how this would transform her future and others she encountered. The reflection resulted in this question, "Have you fulfilled your purpose while you are here on this magnificent planet?" So Diane decided to leave Corporate America to explore her life's purpose to empower others, especially women, to step into their greatness, achieve their dreams faster from a place of clarity on who they are and what they want, with less stress, and enjoy the journey! Diane decided to share 30 years of business leadership experiences and pay-it forward to the next wave of women leaders -- saving them time, removing frustration and helping them avoid obstacles on their journey to the top.

Diane's wish is that we create a culture of honest dialogue, from a place of love and respect that empowers women to leave behind things that hold them back, and amplify the strongest attributes as leaders. For her, it has been a wonderfully enlightening journey, and now as president and CEO of True North Enterprise, she continues her life's journey as an executive transformation coach. Nothing gives Diane more joy than to witness others step into their greatness. It's a unique journey for each individual both personally and professionally. In business, make sure you have the road map, directions, compass and weather forecast to navigate your journey to the top. As Diane always says: "Take great care of yourself, know who you are and what you love, and have a blast changing the world!"

Diane lives in Northern Virginia with her life partner David and has two extraordinary grown children, Samantha and Paul, who are her True North.

Resources

LEADERSHIP LIBRARY

There is no shortage of great books on leadership. Here are many of my favorites that empower leaders to achieve their greatness through transformation. Enjoy them as if they were a box of Godiva chocolates!

1. *Find Your Courage* by Margie Warrell
2. *It's Not a Glass Ceiling, It's a Sticky Floor* by Rebecca Shambaugh
3. *What Men Don't Tell Women About Business* by Christopher V. Flett
4. *Changing the Corporate Landscape* by Jean Otte
5. *Nice Girls Don't Get the Corner Office 101* by Lois P. Frankel, PhD
6. *Ask for It* by Linda Babcock and Sara Lasschever
7. *Women & Leadership* by Barbara Kellerman and Deborah Rhode, Editors
8. *Closing the Leadership Gap* by Marie C. Wilson
9. *When Everything Changed* by Gail Collins
10. *Women, Work & the Art of Savoir Faire* by Mireille Guiliano
11. *Basic Black* by Cathie Black
12. *Why Women Should Rule the World* by Dee Dee Myers
13. *Womenomics* by Claire Shipman and Katty Kay
14. *Tough Choices, A Memoir* by Carly Fiorina
15. *Take the Lead* by Betsey Myers
16. *The Last Word on Power* by Tracy Goss
17. *Beyond Religion* by His Holiness The Dalai Lama
18. *Reinventing Work: The Brand You 50* by Tom Peters
19. *What I Know Now, Letters to My Younger Self* edited by Ellyn Spragins
20. *Women on Top* by Margaret Heffernan
21. *Speak Up!* by Cyndi Maxey, CSP, and Kevin E. O'Connor, CSP

22. *Band of Sisters. American Women at War in Iraq* by Kirsten Holmstedt
23. *The Seven Habits of Highly Effective People* by Stephen R. Covey
24. *What Got You Here Won't Get You There* by Marshall Goldsmith
25. *Emotional Intelligence 2.0* by Travis Bradberry & Jean Greaves
26. *Emotional Intelligence and Social Intelligence* by Daniel Golman
27. *StrengthsFinder 2.0* by Tom Rath
28. *We Are Our Mother's Daughters* by Cokie Roberts
29. *The Articulate Executive* by Granville Toogood
30. *The Purpose Linked Organization* by Alaina Love and Marc Cugnon
31. *Smart Women Finish Rich* by David Bach

Catalyst Pyramids: Women CEOs of the Fortune 1000 (July 17 2012)1
This is a list of women who currently hold CEO positions at companies that
rank on the most recently published Fortune 1000 lists (the Fortune 2012
list). Women currently hold 4.0 percent of Fortune 500 CEO positions
and 4.1 percent of Fortune 1000 CEO positions.

1. Meg Whitman, HP (#10)

2. Virginia Rometty, IBM (#19)

3. Patricia A. Woertz, Archer Daniels Midland Company (ADM) (#28)

4. Indra K. Nooyi, PepsiCo, Inc. (#41)

5. Angela F. Braly, WellPoint, Inc. (#45)

6. Irene B. Rosenfeld, Kraft Foods Inc. (#50)

7. Ellen J. Kullman, DuPont (#72)

8. Carol M. Meyrowitz, The TJX Companies, Inc. (#125)

9. Ursula M. Burns, Xerox Corporation (#127)

10. Sheri S. McCoy, Avon Products Inc. (#234)

11. Deanna M. Mulligan, Guardian (#250)

12. Debra L. Reed, Sempra Energy (#266)

13. Denise M. Morrison, Campbell Soup (#334)

14. Ilene Gordon, Corn Products International (#390)

15. Heather Bresch, Mylan (#396)

16. Kathleen M. Mazzarella, Graybar Electric (#451)

17. Mary Agnes (Maggie) Wilderotter, Frontier Communications (#464)

18. Gracia C. Martore, Gannett (#465)

19. Marissa Mayer, Yahoo (#483)

20. Beth E. Mooney, KeyCorp (#499)

21. Karen W. Katz, The Neiman Marcus Group Inc. (#568)

22. Gretchen McClain, Xylem, (#586)

23. Laura J. Alber, Williams-Sonoma (#596)

24. Patricia Kampling, Alliant Energy (#606)

25. Cindy B. Taylor, Oil States International Inc. (#628)

26. Tamara L. Lundgren, Schnitzer Steel Industries (#631)

27. Kimberly Harris, Puget Sound Energy (#646)

28. Constance H. Lau, Hawaiian Electric Industries Inc. (#659)

29. Mindy F. Grossman, HSN (#665)

30. Amy Miles, Regal Entertainment (#758)

31. Diane M. Sullivan, Brown Shoe Company (#772)

32. Helen McCluskey, Warnaco Inc. (#791)

33. Sandra Cochran, Cracker Barrel (#804)

34. Gayla Delly, Benchmark Electronics (#853)

35. Kay Krill, ANN Inc. (#864)

36. Linda A. Lang, Jack in the Box Inc. (#870)

37. Denise Ramos, ITT (#889)

38. Patti S. Hart, International Game Technology (#918)

39. Judy McReynolds, Arkansas Best Corp. (#944)

40. Debra Cafaro, Ventas (#992)

41. Sara Mathew, Dun & Bradstreet Inc. (#996)

Endnotes

1 Catalyst Research Report, Women CEOs of the Fortune 1000, 2012, accessed on August 19, 2012 from http://www.catalyst.org/publication/271/women-ceos-of-the-fortune-1000

2 Dee Dee Meyers, *Why Women Should Rule the World* (New York: HarperCollins Publishers, 2008).

3 GirlsInc.org. Inspiring all girls to be Strong, Smart & Bold, accessed on July 22, 2012; retrieved from www.girlsinc.org.

4 Myers Briggs.org, *Myers Briggs Type Indicator Descriptions*, 2012, accessed on July 16, 2012, from http://www.myersbriggs.org/my-mbti-personality-type/mbti-basics/the-16-mbti-types.asp.

5 Tom Rath, *StrengthsFinder 2.0.*, 2007, accessed on July 16, 2012 from http://strengths.gallup.com/110440/About-StrengthsFinder-20.aspx.

6 Alaina Love and Marc Cugnon, *The Purpose Linked Organization. Passion Profile Analysis,* 2009, accessed on July 16, 2012, from http://www.thepurposelink.com/passionprofdef.htm.

7 Jean Otte, Founder and CEO of Women Unlimited and author of *Changing the Corporate Landscape,* 2004.

8 Colin Powell decision-making quote, accessed on July 1, 2012, from http://www.theleadershiphub.com/images/leadership-principles-colin-powell.

9 Otte, Jean. (2004) Changing the Corporate Landscape. Little Silver, NJ: Women Unlimited. Copyright 2004. Page 179

10 Wingman (nd). *WordNet® 3.0*, retrieved July 24, 2012, from

Dictionary.com website: http://dictionary.reference.com/browse/wingman.

[11] Women Unlimited, *Leadership Presence: Communicating with Power & Credibility*, 2007, page 2.

[12] Tonya Reiman, *Body Language University. The Human Voice-Pitch*, 2012.

[13] http://www.bodylanguageuniversity.com/public/203.cfm. Retrieved on May 29, 2012.

[14] Christopher Flett, *What Men Don't Tell Women about Business* (Hoboken, NJ: John Wiley & Sons, 2008), page 57.

[15] ThinkExist.com Quotations, "Maya Angelou quotes," ThinkExist. com Quotations Online, June 1, 2012 from http://en.thinkexist. com/quotes/maya_angelou/.

[16] Wikipedia.org, *Robert Plutchik, accessed on August 18, 2012, from* http://en.wikipedia.org/wiki/Robert_Plutchik.

[17] The Vanguard Group, *Are Women Better Investors than Men?* accessed on July 10, 2012, from https://retirementplans.vanguard.com/VGApp/pe/pubnews/WomenBetterInvestors.jsf.

[18] Claire Shipman and Katty Kay, *Womenomics* (New York: HarperCollins Publishers, 2009). Hans Phillips, Accomplishment Coaching, 2008.

[19] Catalyst.org, *Women CEOs of the Fortune 1000,* accessed on July 16, 2012, from http://www.catalyst.org/publication/271/women-ceos-of-the-fortune-1000.

[20] National Center for Education Statistics quoting statistics from US Department of Education, National Center for Education Statistics. *Digest of Education Statistics, 2010* (NCES 2011-015), 2011, Chapter 3, accessed on July 16, 2012, from http://nces.ed.gov/fastfacts/display.asp?id=98.

[21] Claire Shipman and Katty Kay, *Womenomics* (New York: HarperCollins Publishers, 2009).

[22] Catalyst Research Report, *Women Entrepreneurs: Why Companies Lose Female Talent and What They Can Do About It*, 2009, accessed on July 16, 2012 from http://www.catalyst.org/publication/76/women-entrepreneurs-why-companies-lose-female-talent-and-what-they-can-do-about-it.

[23] American Express Open, *State of Women-Owned Businesses Report. A Summary of Important Trends, 1997–2011.* 2012, accessed on July 16, 2012, from WomenReport_Final.pdf. (p.2). http://www.openforum.com/articles/2012-american-express-open-state-of-women-owned-businesses-report.